FUNNY BONES

A Day in the Life of a Healer – Short Story Series

Book 1 of 4

Carolle Jean-Murat MD.

Published by Hibiscus Productions

Editing by Karyn Louise Wilkening, Expert Editing, Ink.
ISBN: 1580150586
ISBN 13: 9781580150583
Library of Congress Control Number: 2017951880
Hibiscus Productions, La Mesa, CA

DEDICATION

This book is dedicated to my patients and all who have been with me through this wonderful journey of life.

TABLE OF CONTENTS

INTRODUCTION

Throughout my life I kept a detailed personal journal, and decided to use humorous and unusual incidents from it to create this mini book for my readers. You're invited to join me on my adventures in Haiti, Mexico, Jamaica, Canada, Germany, and around the US. I'm happy to share these special, often funny, moments from my very full life... and sincerely hope this little book helps inspire you to enjoy YOUR life to the fullest!

Some of my readers are familiar with my background and unusual family life in Haiti from my other books, appearances and lectures. But for those of you who are not, here are the highlights...

I was born in Port-au-Prince, the capital of Haiti, in 1950, the first-born daughter of Joseph Karl

Jean, and Marie Anne Lamercie Murat. My mother's father Mirabeau Murat, one of the best-known Voodoo priests and indigenous healers in Haiti, lived in Bizoton, a small town outside Port-au-Prince. I called him Grand-Père. My mother was a midwife and herbalist, and no one Mother's family had ever graduated from primary school.

In contrast, my father came from a family where being a lawyer, judge or teacher was the norm. My paternal grandfather was a pharmacist, and an alcoholic. Due to his father's abusive behavior, my father left home as a teenager to fend for himself. He met my mother when he was twenty-four and she was twenty, and they soon married.

When I was four years old and my baby sister Marise was two, my parents separated, and Mother, Marise, and I went to live in my Grand-Père's healing compound in Bizoton. But Father demanded that my sister and I go to live with his mother, who we called Grandma, and Julia her older sister, called Tatante, away from the "bad" influence of Voodoo on my mother's side of the family.

Mother refused to let us go, then found herself pregnant with twins and plagued with severe pains, no longer able to work as a seamstress to feed us. There were no social programs to help impoverished women with small children in Haiti, so Grandma finally convinced Mother to let my sister and I live with her and Tatante; she would take care of us, and we would have an opportunity to get a good education. Mother made the biggest sacrifice a mother could make and reluctantly agreed.

The societal class system was so strong that the prestigious Catholic school I attended eventually kicked me out when they learned about my maternal origins. My maternal grandfather, Mirabeau, the well-known indigenous Voodoo healer, was considered evil by the Catholic Church. Over the years, the impact of this constant discrimination, secrecy and turmoil in my family tore me apart, and caused me to become very ill. Grandma took me to many medical doctors, but they were unsuccessful in improving my health. My mother, upon learning I was very ill, insisted on taking me to my Grand-Père Mirabeau, the Voodoo priest. It was his indigenous healing skill that restored my health, which made a very great impression on me.

Having to live in a society that consistently denied a part of me only increased my determination to succeed. During my occasional visits to Grand-Père Mirabeau, he reassured me that I would be a healer like him, but that because of my paternal family's influence and help, I would acquire the skill in formal medical school. He promised me that he would always be available for "second opinions."

1965 PORT-AU-PRINCE, HAITI

CHILDHOOD SURGICAL SKILLS

There were many lessons I had to learn as a little girl living in Grandma's strict household. She was adamant that I learn to cook, sew, and especially learn to wash underwear so they were always clean.

"What would you do if you fainted or were involved in an accident, with dirty underwear on?" she would ask. I also had to learn to iron without getting burned; a big chore since it was a hollow metal contraption with a flat bottom, into which you stuffed burning charcoal.

One summer night in my early teens, Grandma told me to make sure that I reserved the next two days to learn how to kill a chicken and have it ready for dinner. I did not like this idea, but had no choice.

The next day, it was with apprehension that I had to watch the chicken from our yard killed. "She is all yours now," Grandma said. Under her guidance, I dipped it for a few seconds in a pot of boiling water and rapidly plucked the large feathers. Then, using newspapers that I threw on an open fire pit made of burning charcoal, I grabbed the neck and its two feet and gently waved it over the flame to remove the fine feathers.

Grandma then handed me a knife, so I could neatly cut the limbs and then open the abdomen, like a surgeon. "Be careful," she said, guiding my trembling hands and giving me back the big sharp knife that kept on falling out of them. "You have to make sure you do this precisely, so you don't cut the guts, especially the gallbladder. A ruptured gallbladder with its green liquid would mean a spoiled dinner."

Another day, Grandma gave me a large piece of fabric that she had purposely cut up with scissors for me to repair and patch. "You never know," she said. "Your husband may one day lose his job, or he may disappear because the authorities don't like him, or he may get killed. You don't want your children to walk the streets of Port-au-Prince with raggedy clothes." So I learned how to sew and do fine stitches and other skills.

When Grandma was teaching you something, especially when she knew you disliked it but she felt that it was "good for your future as a well-prepared young woman," she accepted no complaints. She didn't have to say anything; she would just give you that "look" and you'd know you had to shut up.

Little did I know that *every single thing* Grandma forced me to learn as a child would become very handy in the future, when I became not only a doctor but also an ob-gyn surgeon.

1966 GONAIVES, HAITI

THE BACK COUNTRY, A BOY, AND A BIKE

Eventually my mother met Achilles, an accountant for the CARE Foundation in Port-au-Prince. The Foundation distributed wheat and white flour, powdered milk, crushed oats, and cooking oil to the poor. Finding that poor people were sometimes too proud to come and get the food, Achilles found something in each small town he visited that needed to be fixed. He then hired unemployed people to make the repairs, and paid them with food.

This kind man fell in love with Mother, promising to take care of her and be a father to Fifi, my younger sister. I liked Achilles the first time I met him. He was skinny, tall, with a light brown complexion and light brown eyes. He told my sister Marise and me that we could consider him a father since ours had escaped into exile in America. We all agreed to call him "Pappy." Now Mother had in her life someone who loved her and cared for her. It was the first time I had seen her so happy.

Achilles was transferred to Gonaives, a town on the northern Haitian coastline where he had gone to primary school, to become director of the Northern division of the CARE Foundation. Gonaives was a very famous town that played a major role during the Revolutionary War for independence against France. It was in Gonaives, after the war, that the generals got together on January 1, 1804, to proclaim Haiti's independence – the first free black country in the new world! Achilles asked Mother to spend the summer of 1966 in Gonaives.

Marise and I, still living with Grandma, were very excited to spend a whole vacation with our mother for the first time. We would be staying in a small town on the outskirts of Gonaives. Dates grown in the area were exported to other countries. Along our street many date trees stood tall. The furnished house had three bedrooms, running water and electricity. The water came from a well in the back yard, with the help of an electric pump. When there was a blackout, the water was pulled by hand. Across the street was a small chicken, goat, and pig farm, and next to it was a sugar cane field.

On a street by our house, a few people gathered during the day to sell fruits, sugar cane, and housewares. Three blocks away was an abandoned railway station and nearby, a factory where lemon oil was produced. A tangy aroma filled the air because the drainage from the factory ran down a ditch in front of our house. A green sludgy mixture filled much of the ditch, which was so big that a bridge wide enough to allow the passage of a car, connected our front yard to the street.

We went to visit Achilles' Aunt Georgette, who lived in a nice house like ours in the affluent area of Gonaives. That's where I met Eden, Achilles' nephew. Eden was eighteen, and the most handsome young man I had ever met. He went to school in Port au Prince but spent his vacations back in Gonaives.

I had no interest in boys except as friends. "Decent girls" in Haiti didn't date until they were out of college. Because Mother had gotten pregnant at twenty, married Father, and bore me one month later, Tatante always made me feel that Mother was a loose girl who had trapped Father with children and had then been abandoned. I decided that would *never* happen to me I'd be celibate all my life, and never have children. I would stay away from men, and they would stay away from me.

Anyway, how could I date anyone? My friends never knew about Mother and her family's Voodoo connection. I wondered what I would do if I did want to date. How would I tell his parents about Mother's family?

But I found myself attracted to Eden. Maybe the attraction was because I thought he was safe. His uncle was with Mother without shame. But would Grandma think Eden was good enough for me? I decided to stay away from Eden. I was going to be in Gonaives for only two months. I would go back to Port au Prince and that would be it.

But, every afternoon Eden came to visit, riding his bike. He brought me books and records. Everyone teased me about it.

In Gonaives, as in most small towns, bicycles were the major mode of transportation. I had never seen a girl ride a bike until I came to Gonaives. In Port au Prince, the boys I knew used bicycles as toys, and only poor people who couldn't afford cars used bikes for transportation.

Since I was always a bit contrary, I got it in my head that I wanted to learn how to ride one. Eden happily offered to be my teacher, and Achilles agreed to rent a bike for me.

For days in the paved front yard Eden patiently taught me how to keep my balance and learn to steer. Soon I told him I didn't need him anymore, that I could do it without him. I rode away from him, over the bridge, as fast as I could. The next thing I knew, I was in that green water ditch. The vendors across the street laughed. So did Eden. I never felt so embarrassed, especially in front of him.

I ran into the house full of shame, aching all over. But I took a shower, put on clean clothes, ran back outside, jumped on the bicycle to ride again to prove to everyone, including myself, that I could do it.

I didn't realize how much I was hurt until getting into bed that night. The skin on both knees was cracked open. By the next day, there was infection, and I had to stay in bed. Achilles came home with a doctor, Frederique, the son of Grandma's lawyer cousin. Frédérique had gone to l'École de Médecine in Port au Prince. He and his father often came to visit us when they were in town. I told Dr. Frederique that I wanted some day to be a doctor.

"That's a very good idea," he told me. "But remember that it is a lot of hard work," I told him I knew that it was going to be a long battle, but I was ready for it.

The doctor gave me some shots, which I hated. He told us the cuts got infected from the filth in the ditch. For days, I walked around with a sore bottom. My forearm, where I got a Tetanus shot, was the most painful. It took days to get better.

I was mad Eden had laughed at me, and refused to see him again. I'd show him and everyone else! I got on the bike and practiced by myself without any problems. Since there was nothing much else to do, I began waiting in front of the house for a cyclist to pass by, and then tailgate him. It was never a girl, of course.

When one guy realized I was trying to race, he took the challenge and sped up. The race was on, and continued until he got passed by a girl! You should have seen the look on his face.

1972 NEW YORK CITY

SPEAKING UP FOR MYSELF

I was twenty when I set aside my dream of going to school in Europe. Instead, if I went to the Autonomous University of Guadalajara School of Medicine in Mexico, recognized by the US, I could apply for a student loan after the first year. The loan would be enough to pay for tuition and books. The rest would have to come from Father, any savings I had, and by working during semester breaks. So, I had to start making some money.

Living in New York City with Father's help, I was looking for a job when I was referred to the United States Research and Development (USR&D), in lower Manhattan. There was an eight-week program where low-income people without jobs could learn a skill and get paid $40 a week. The objective was to train people, get them off welfare, get them to work, and increase their self-esteem. They would be turned into skilled, productive, tax-paying citizens.

I was accepted by the program and by the time it ended, I was typing seventy words a minute. I learned how to take an exam for a clerical job, and how to conduct myself during a job interview. When I had time I ventured around NYC, went to the Planetarium, and one night to Broadway to see "Pearly," starring Melba Moore. There was a fashion show for graduation, and I was one of the models. It was the first time I felt good about being six feet tall!

Then I worked at RCA for three months until it would be time to go to Mexico. I developed a warm friendship with everyone around. I did my work quickly and found time to chat with the engineers. But the job got boring for me. I was more interested in the engineers' work, and in picking up languages.

I started to learn Chinese from Mr. Chin at work. I practiced my Spanish with the head of the department, Mr. Cifuentes, who was from Columbia. His secretary, Jody, had just emigrated from Israel and one day asked me if I would teach her French during the fifteen-minute break we had every afternoon.

"I will teach you French if you teach me Hebrew," I told her. In no time, I learned the Hebrew alphabet and how to write basic sentences. Some of the engineers thought I was crazy. "Why in the world would you learn Hebrew?" My answer to these kinds of questions was always, "Why not?"

One day, I was talking to one of the managers in his office when he asked, "What's an intelligent girl like you doing in a job like this? Do you know that when I put plans together, I'm confident there won't be mistakes because I know that you'll catch them and come to bug me?" I told him about my big plans to go to medical school. He was very pleased and gave me a big hug, telling me he knew I'd be a great doctor.

A week before I was to leave for Mexico, I was notified that one necessary paper was missing; it would take at least two months to get it from Haiti. Now I had to wait another year to go to medical school.

After feeling sorry for myself for a short while, it was time to look for another job. I heard about an opening at the USR&D headquarters in the Gulf and Western Plaza in Manhattan. The job was to help a writer put together a manual for Hispanic students learning English as a second language. I would type and edit at the same time. All I needed was a background in Spanish and good typing skills.

The manual had to be finished in three months. I thought the job was perfect for me, figuring I knew enough Spanish to do well. By then I was typing eighty words a minute.

I took a bus, and then a train, got off at 42nd street, then took another train. The tall building had a giant G & W glowing at the top. I got to the nineteenth floor and told the receptionist I had an appointment to apply for a job. I sat to wait by the large glass window and could see skaters below twirling around an ice rink. People looked very small from way up there.

I was startled by a huge black man wearing a beret, whom the receptionist asked to show me the way to my appointment.

"Follow me, Ma'am," he said. "My name is Larry, and I'm pleased to meet you." He had a quiet voice, not what I expected from such a giant. The personnel department was just around the corner. Larry, who I learned later was a Muslim, accompanied me to the correct door.

Inside the office I met a blonde lady named Cindy Rosenberg, according to the nameplate on her desk.

"I'm here to apply for the position with Mr. Rodriguez," I told her. She wanted to know about my bilingual experience. I told her I knew how to write very well in both basic English and Spanish.

"It's not only writing," she said. "There is some editing involved." I replied that I thought I could handle it.

"By the way, which other languages do you speak?" she asked. I told her that I grew up speaking French and Haitian Kréyol, and then learned Spanish in preparation for going to Medical School in Mexico. I also said that I learned to speak a little Hebrew.

"How did you learn how to speak Hebrew? Why? What do you know?" she asked me with a puzzled look on her face. I told her that I had learned the alphabet, the writing, and pronunciation of a few sentences that could help me get by. That I had learned just for the fun of it.

"And how long did it take you to learn all this?" she asked me.

"Three months," I told her. "During a fifteen-minute work break each afternoon."

"You have the job," she said, nodding. "If you could learn that much Hebrew in so little time, you can do anything. By the way, I'm from Israel," she added with a smile.

My new boss, Mr. Rodriguez, was a delight. He was from Spain, an aspiring theatrical actor. On the side, he did any job to get by. He gave me free tickets to see him play Don Juan in a small theater. I told him he was very good, and not just because he was my boss!

"I'll be on Broadway someday," he told me. "And I'll make sure you get free tickets."

Soon I met the other twenty people who worked at USR&D and became friends with most of them, like Tony the accountant, Carol in payroll, Ruth, and Inga in purchasing, and Mary, the receptionist. Part of my job was to answer the phone when Mary was out to lunch, and help anyone who needed typing done.

One day Mr. Rodriguez told me he was looking for someone to help him with some illustrations for the manuals. I told him that I had a good background in drawing. "It's not so simple," he told me. He had written some short stories, and I would have to read them one by one to come up with appropriate illustrations. I convinced him to let me try. For a story about Christopher Columbus, I drew three flagships. He was very satisfied and told me I could stay after the manual was finished, to do the illustrations for the stories. That would pay me for another two or three weeks!

I had been at this job a short time when I noticed John Williams, the vice president. His job was to put proposals together and send them to Washington, the Capitol, the House of Representatives, and the Department of Education and Welfare. He was the one who had written and received a grant for the program through which I had learned my secretarial skills. His philosophy was that if you teach a skill to an unemployed person on welfare, the person could enter the work force, become a tax-paying citizen, and be able to pay back the money invested.

My desk was in the hallway, facing Mr. Williams' office. I sat between his secretary and Nancy, who assisted Mr. Haddad, the president, and Ms. Rosenberg. Nancy thought she was a big shot and didn't talk to anyone unless she was giving orders.

Mr. Williams, the vice president, was always in a bad mood. He came into the office every morning with a cigarette in his mouth, and never said good morning. I didn't think he even noticed me. I had been working for a week when Kathy, his secretary of two weeks, came out of his office in tears, Mr. Williams right behind her, cursing, telling her to get out!

The scoop about Mr. Williams was that no one had ever worked for him for more than two weeks. He was very smart and brought in money to keep the company going, so everyone had to tolerate his bad attitude. But the proposals that Mr. Williams put together had to get to Washington on strict timelines. Until they could find a secretary – who would eventually quit after two weeks – a typist had to be found to help him. One proposal had to be sent to Washington in two days. Nancy asked me if I was willing to work overtime to finish it. She would have big Larry stay with me and take me to the subway station if I had to stay long into the evenings. I did not like the idea of working for such an ogre, but I would get four dollars an hour, and overtime would be paid at six dollars an hour! So I agreed.

I spent my days at USR&D working with Mr. Rodriguez, answering the telephone, and staying overtime to type proposals for Mr. Williams whenever he fired his secretaries. Other companies contracted with USR&D to find employees on the weekend to review their computer printouts. I was asked one day if I would like to make some extra money. The answer was always, "Yes, please," so I could afford medical school.

So, every other Sunday, I went to various locations in Manhattan to work the whole day, with one hour off for lunch, comparing computer cards against a big list. The pay was $3 an hour, good money then. The subway cost thirty cents, a large pastrami sandwich cost ninety cents, and a large coke, thirty cents. My paycheck was $18 after tax.

Carol in payroll was responsible for hiring employees and supervising them on Sundays. She did not like the idea of spending time away from her family, even though she made extra money for Sunday. I asked her if I could help. She made me responsible for finding the twenty employees needed. In return, I got $3.50 an hour. I had no problem finding employees! My sisters Marise and Fifi, friend Nicole and her two sisters, two distant cousins, and some of my sister's classmates were more than happy to work!

Mr. Williams fired another secretary before another deadline and, of course, I would be the one to finish the proposal. That night, I realized that in less than two weeks my time on my contract work would be up, and I'd have to look for another job.

I had an idea: I was more knowledgeable than any secretary that Mr. Williams would ever have. I knew everything about the outside jobs and the proposals. If I worked for *him*, I could take over Carol's position and double my money on Sundays. But I'd have to find a way to deal with him, knowing he had never even thanked me for working overtime and putting his proposals together on time.

That's it, I thought, I'm going to work for Mr. Williams and make more money for medical school tuition and could send more money to Mother. I started rehearsing how to approach Mr. Williams. I reminded myself of Grandma telling me I should never be afraid of any other person. "We are all the same. We all go to the toilet."

I was at my desk the next morning when he stalked past me into his office with a cup of coffee and a cigarette, ignoring me as usual. I took a deep breath and knocked at his door. "Mr. Williams, I would like to speak with you."

"What do you want? I don't have time to waste," he answered angrily.

"May I please come in?" I said shyly.

"You may, but be brief."

"Mr. Williams, I want to work for you," I told him. That shocked him, and he just stared at me. He had beautiful blue eyes, a small mustache, but was otherwise clean-shaven. I could see that he had suffered from acne when he was young, judging from his scarred lower face. I realized he wasn't as intimidating as I thought. I told him that I was planning to go to medical school in six months and that my job at USR&D was going to be over in two weeks. I needed to save as much money as possible.

"Since I'm the one who has done most of the proposals for the past three months, I will accept working for you on one condition: no yelling at me," I said, gaining confidence. "I will respect you as much as you respect me. I promise to do my best. If I make a mistake, call me to your office, tell me so, and then fire me. But don't scream at me in front of the whole company."

Probably no employee had ever talked to him as I did. He finally looked at me and said, "We will give it a try." I left his office holding my mouth so I wouldn't scream. With a mischievous smile on my face, I started to clean my desk and move my possessions to Mr.

Williams' secretary's desk. I told Nancy that from then on, I took orders only from Mr. Williams. She looked at me with startled eyes.

"Yes," I told her, "from now on I am Mr. Williams' secretary."

Mr. Williams and I developed a good working relationship. Soon I took over Carol's job on Sundays. The first day at this new job, I gathered my workmates and told them that I was the boss now. I never had any problems with them. New contracts were made between USR&D and other companies for clerical jobs. That summer, I was able to find full-time jobs for Nicole, my sisters, and most of my Sunday employees. Soon, Haitian friends were calling me trying to find jobs. Father boasted to his friends that his daughter was able to give jobs to hundreds of people.

I had been working for Mr. Williams for over two months, with everything going very smoothly. He told me before leaving for lunch that upon his return he would be in need of a phone number that should have been in a letter I recently sent to Texas. I had made a bad mistake. I panicked, gobbling Maalox instead of lunch. Everyone felt sorry for me, expecting Mr. Williams to blow the place apart. When he returned, I went bravely to his office and told him what had happened. I said that it was okay if he fired me.

"Don't worry," he told me, looking on his desk pad. "You know, I have the bad habit of scribbling phone numbers while talking, probably it's here. Oh, there it is," he said to me, while I was on the brink of fainting. I left the office while Mr. Williams dialed the number. Everybody was in shock when they saw me coming out of his office smiling. I told them what had happened, and soon became the only person people came to when they had to deal with Mr. Williams.

At that time, there was no such thing as overnight mail. On three different occasions, proposals from our office had to be hand delivered at the last minute. I was the one who took them to Washington, DC, the Capitol, the House of Representatives, the Department of Health Education and Welfare, all expenses paid.

I felt strange at first among businessmen taking the charter from La Guardia Airport. By the second trip, however, I had the hang of it and made sure I bought a copy of the New York Times to read on the plane, just like everyone else. People looked surprised when such a young black woman stopped in fancy restaurants for lunch, left nice tips, and requested receipts.

One day, Mr. Williams called me into his office to thank me for working for him. His wife had noticed that he was in a better mood when he came home, and that he had cut down on smoking. Mr. Williams actually said that he was going to miss me.

Since I had only two more weeks to work at USR&D, I decided to speak up while he was in this good mood and request something unusual. I wanted to take a week off for traveling and registering before starting school. I took a deep breath and asked Mr. Williams to give me the last week of July off, with pay, as a gift for medical school.

"It is not company policy," he said. "An employee has to work a full year to get one week of vacation. No employee has ever been given leave with pay during short employment."

"Mr. Williams," I told him. "You do not realize the power that you have in this company. You are its brain. You are the one who brings in the money. I bet no one would dare contradict you if you write a memo saying that because of the excellent job I've done for you, you're requesting an exception for me."

Speaking up for myself worked! I got my week off with full pay!

1972 BROOKLYN, NEW YORK

FIRST KISS

Father's girlfriend, Eka, was a beautiful woman from Haiti who treated us like we were her own daughters. Eka had an older sister, Fernande, who married a gentleman named Fernand. I called them the "Fernandos." They lived in upper Manhattan. They told wonderful stories about our native land and introduced me to many interesting people, including Reynold, Fernand's younger brother.

Reynold was studying economic science in Paris and was on vacation in New York. He was about six-foot-four, handsome, well-built, wore glasses, and had a short beard. I was wearing a two-piece mini-skirt when I met him, and I noticed he kept looking at my legs.

"Are you a model?" he asked me. "You look so nice." I figured he was teasing me. A typical man, I thought to myself. He had zeroed in on something I was sensitive about. Tatante and my friends always told me that I walked like a duck, so I did not see myself as somebody who had nice legs, like a model.

"Oh yeah," I replied sarcastically. "That's what I do for a living." But he persisted, and I eventually told Reynold about my dreams of becoming a doctor and my plans to go to Guadalajara. Reynold and I spent lots of time talking on the phone while he was vacationing in New York. When he left, we agreed to keep writing to each other. I wrote to Reynold to tell him he would have a nice, well-paying job waiting for him when he came back to New York.

Reynold came back from Paris wanting to spend a lot of time with me and eventually trying to give me kisses. I mentioned the situation to Eka, who commented that something was wrong with me for refusing him. I was twenty-one, about to start medical school in Mexico, and was not interested in boys. In fact, I had never kissed one. I didn't think I was weird, but I wondered if Eka was right and if I would ever let a man near me.

I was at home when Father called. He was dating another woman and wanted me to visit her. I told him it was in bad taste and I did not want to be involved with his dirty life. He said that he was very proud of me and wanted me to meet the love of his life before I left for Guadalajara. That's how I was forced to meet Marie, who believed Father was celibate and living with his three daughters. I wished that I could tell her to stay away from Father, but I didn't dare.

Father told me that he would be home late that night. I knew he would be with Marie. Meanwhile, Eka came home from work sick with the flu, running a high fever.

"Why don't you go to bed and rest?" I asked her.

"No," she said. "I have to cook for your father."

"He's going to come home late," I told her. "He might not even be hungry. And you should be resting." Eka didn't listen to me. She fixed rice, beans, beef with mixed vegetables, and Jello, then collapsed into bed. Father finally came home around ten o'clock, walked to the kitchen, looked at the food on the stove, and said "I don't want dinner. Where is Eka?"

"She's sleeping," I told him. "She has been very sick."

"Tell her that I want some Jello."

"Why don't you get your own Jello?" I exploded. Here was a man who had been having fun with a different woman while his sick girlfriend had prepared a full meal he did not even have the decency to eat. Now he wanted her to get out of bed to give him some Jello? Eka was awakened by the loud voices and walked like a zombie into the kitchen. I ran toward her and pushed her back toward her room. You're not going to give this man any Jello." Eka did not know what to do. She could tell I was seriously upset.

"That's okay," Father told her. "I'll get my own." Laughing, he opened the refrigerator, and served himself. I yelled at him, telling him what I thought of him, his selfishness, his insensitivity toward women. Father smiled at me, sat down at the dining room table, and ate the Jello. I ran to my room to cry. Now I was *sure* I wanted to be celibate the rest of my life.

One day Reynold invited me to see *The Godfather* at a movie theater not far from Flatbush Avenue and I agreed to accompany him. Eka told me in no uncertain terms that I should let him kiss me after the movie; otherwise, *she would not let me back in the house.* I very reluctantly promised I would try. We went to the movie but I couldn't focus on it at all. My mind was paralyzed on the idea of a potential first kiss.

Back at my house, I was standing in the hallway by the staircase with Reynold, and my heart was pounding. He told me he wanted me to be his girlfriend. I didn't answer. I was in a state of panic! He held me against him and leaned in to kiss me. I closed my eyes, hoping I would disappear. After his lips brushed mine, I ran upstairs, with Reynold following me, and quickly opened the door.

Eka was sitting in the living room, knitting. She looked up at my shocked and panicked face, and knew I had finally let him kiss me.

"*Entrez, s'il vous plait,*" she told us with a big, mischievous smile.

1974 GUADALAJARA, MEXICO

JUST LIKE BRILLO!

When I left Haiti in 1970 bound for the US, I was twenty years old and had big dreams. I hoped to be accepted into medical school at a French-speaking university in Europe. I dreamed of returning to Haiti as a doctor to be able to help the poor people. When I arrived in the US with my sisters Marise and Fifi, my plan was to stay in New York for only a few months. I did not have the opportunity to go to medical school in Europe as I planned but ended up two years later with my friend Nicole at the Autonomous University of Guadalajara School of Medicine in Mexico. I started on August 4, 1972.

American students who studied at the UAG had a path different from students from Latin America and the Caribbean who wanted to do postgraduate training in the US. Many did not like the rigors of studying in Spanish, and for the first time in their lives had a taste of prejudice. White males who came from rich families had to wait in line like everybody else, and the color of their skin did not give them an automatic advantage. At the University, what counted most was being able to speak Spanish.

Speaking many languages made me very popular with the other students. I helped them with their homework, giving me another opportunity to pay my way through medical school. One of the white students in my group was Bill, and we became good friends. We hung around together for a long time. He wanted to date me, but I refused, and he accused ME of being prejudiced.

One day I was wearing my hair naturally as an Afro, although most of the time I would press my kinky hair to make it more manageable.

"May I touch your hair?" Bill asked me politely.

"No problem, go ahead." He hesitated at first, then touched my hair gently.

"I knew it, I knew it," he said with a smile. "Just like Brillo!"

"My father would die if he knew that my best friend is a black woman," he added… and we laughed hysterically.

1976 BROOKLYN, NEW YORK

MULTILINGUAL HEALING

While working in New York at RCA Global Communication with many engineers from all over the world, not only did I learn Hebrew, I also started to learn Polish. Many in the department made fun of me for bothering, but little did they know that the few words I learned would come in handy someday.

While doing my internal medicine rotation, I had to take care of an elderly diabetic man who was found unconscious with no ID in the streets. We thought that he may have had a stroke. No one was able to communicate with him.

An idea came to me to try speaking to him in the other languages I knew. I tried a few and when I said in Polish "*Dzień dobry. Jak się masz?*" (Good morning, how are you?), he answered me! "*Mam się dobrze dziękuję I,*" ("I am good, thank you") he replied with a big smile. Oh, the power of knowing other languages.

Three days later when his family located him, we were so very happy. With one of them translating, he told me how much it meant to him to see my smile while he was lying there in the hospital bed worried about his family and unable to communicate with anyone.

I also learned how grateful many Poles were towards my people because during World War II, Haiti was one of the few countries offering refuge to any Pole fleeing from Germany.

The relationship started during our slave revolution in the early 19th century that would end with Haiti becoming the second independent state on January 1, 1804, after the US, and the first country in the Western hemisphere, and the only one in the world, made of slaves who fought their masters and won.

Napoleon recruited 50,000 men from Europe to fight and among them were 5,000 Poles, most of whom died during battles or from tropical diseases. However, the Poles believed in freedom against oppression and soon joined the Haitians in their wars for freedom. After the revolution in my country, many were naturalized as Haitian citizens by General Jean-Jacques Dessalines, one of our war heroes and the first Haitian head of state.

1977 TEPUXTLA, SINALOA, MEXICO

IMMERSION IN THE PUEBLOS

To be accepted into a medical postgraduate program in the US as I planned, I needed to spend a year interning at an accredited hospital, and another year of social services with the Department of Public Health in Mexico.

After I spent my year of internship at the University of the West Indies in Jamaica in 1976, my social services assignment was to a small Mexican town called Tepuxtla, about an hour bus ride from Mazatlán. I would be the first doctor ever in this small village of less than nine hundred people. Soon, I would learn that following the priest and schoolteachers, a doctor is the most important person in such a village.

Arrangements were made for me to stay with a family in their two-bedroom house with a living room and small kitchen. The toilet and cold-water shower were outside in the yard. I could use the sparsely-furnished living room as my consult room and pharmacy. The covered patio in front of the house would serve as my waiting room.

On occasion, I had the opportunity to make house calls on foot to surrounding villages. To make house calls when it wasn't raining, I was able to cross the river El Recodo, famous for *La Banda del Recodo*, a band with the same name.

About two miles before you reach Tepuxtla from Mazatlán, there is another small village called La Barrigona. I was assigned to go there on Thursdays to give health classes to young girls and to see a patient or two. I spent the time at the make-shift clinic in the home of Lupe Chavarría. I mostly saw their friends and family members since very few people came from the Pueblo. They were too afraid of their local *curandera*, who let them know that anyone who saw the medical doctor would be cursed!

When I had time, I would spend it with Doña Isabel, who taught me how to prepare Mexican-style dishes, especially her famous tamales *"estilo Sinaloense."*

It was a family affair. We used either chicken or pork that was well-seasoned and cooked it slowly with its own juice. I would add some of the things I had learned from Grandma to make it even tastier. We would buy the masa freshly made at the *tortillería* and mix it with lard and salt. On the side, we cut canned olives, carrots, sweet peppers, and potatoes into small slices. First, we laid a few tablespoons of masa on a bed made of corn leaves, then added the meat, the cut vegetables, a few raisins, and then bathed them with juice from the meat, rolled them, and placed them on a steamer.

Doña Isabel taught me so well that I became famous for my tamales, and whenever I would visit any other Mexican towns, a day would be put aside so *Doctora Carolina* would make her *"tamales estilo Sinaloense."*

During this time, musician Jose Maria Napoleón was very famous. I had met him in 1973 in Celaya, in the state of Guanajuato, when I went with a fellow student to a family member's house, and he was visiting and serenading in their backyard. His song, *Hombre*, was played all the time on the radio. The lyrics of that song translated to: "Man, if you say you are a man, do not interrupt your journey. Otherwise, this life is just a grave dwelling. Even a rose comes with its thorn. If you do not know pain, you will not know the joy."

That song of his seemed like the story of my life, always going forward in spite of the obstacles, taking life head on, not being afraid to get up when I would fall.

As Grandma always said," if you are riding a horse in the middle of nowhere and you fall off, when you finally realize where you are, you can only see the hind legs of your horse in the dust, far, far away. You look above and see the bright sun and vultures hovering over you, waiting to feast upon your carcass. You then have no choice but to get up and keep on walking."

Against many obstacles I made the best of my situation and lived with the people of these Pueblo communities as a friend, family member, sister, confidante, and doctor.

One of our pastimes was to watch *telenovelas*, the infamous soap opera, with many of the villagers crowding the Gonzales living room. They had the only television in town. We would cry and laugh together, pointing fingers and cursing the evil protagonists.

Another pastime was to gather on Sunday afternoons at the main *plazuela*. The mothers would bring chairs and make a large circle. The girls would make a circle and walk one way, while the guys made another circle and walked the other way. When a man would come face to face with the woman he loved, they would just smile at each other. Sometimes, they would dance, putting a peso in the old *electrola* (jukebox). When it was time to dance, I'd always join in. At six feet I was the tallest in the whole town, but I had all the gorgeous young men teaching me to keep the beat of *la música norteña*.

Lupe would tease me when I would go to La Barrigona on Thursdays and say that I was now talking like the people of Tepuxtla. Totally immersing myself as one of their own and having a good ear for languages… it was bound to happen.

1978 MILWAUKEE, WISCONSIN

A HAITIAN BUSH WOMAN HAS TO EAT!

It was when I was accepted for postgraduate training in obstetrics and gynecology at Mount Sinai Medical Center in Milwaukee, Wisconsin, where I nearly froze to death, never worked so hard, or ate so little. Being a first-year resident meant having no more status than a pile of dirt!

When on call, which was every third night, I would leave my home at 6 AM and not return until the next day after 5 PM, without sleeping and barely eating.

Any time I asked why we all had to work to the breaking point, I was told, "it's just the way it is."

"But it's worse than slavery," I would say. "At least my ancestors were allowed to sleep and eat."

Nothing changed at work for me until I made a very scary declaration.

I had heard about a plane a few years earlier carrying the Uruguayan rugby team on the way to Chile that crashed into the Andes Mountains. The survivors turned to cannibalism to survive until they were saved after seventy-two days.

With that horror in mind I said: "I can handle being expected to be in three places at the same time; the labor and delivery ward, the emergency room, and the floors doing admissions, *but I have to eat* – I'm a Haitian bush woman, and if I don't eat... *you may find one of your patients with an ear missing.*" After that shocking statement, whenever I asked for a little time to get some food, no one dared say anything!

1980 MILWAUKEE, WISCONSIN

ANESTHESIOLOGIST OR OBSTETRICIAN?

A residency in obstetrics and gynecology is a four-year program, and at the end a doctor takes a one-day written exam to become board eligible. Then, after one year in private practice, there are certain criteria of how many obstetrical and gynecological surgical cases must be accumulated to take an oral exam. Passing that oral exam would designate me to be board-certified and be a Diplomate of the American College of Obstetrician and Gynecologist. I could then apply to become a Fellow of the American College of Obstetrics and Gynecology. At that point, I would be known as

Carolle Jean-Murat, M.D., F.A.C.O.G – the respected title that was my goal.

To take my oral board, I needed to arrange eighteen months each of obstetric training and gynecological training. Always having in the back of my mind that I may one day go back to Haiti, I wanted to take advantage of getting a well-rounded education that would complement the excellent training I had in Jamaica.

I devised a plan where I would spend two months at St. Mary Hospital doing obstetrical anesthesia associated with the Medical College of Wisconsin; four months of infertility (two at the University of Madison, Wisconsin and at the University of California Los Angeles; four months in high-risk obstetrics; and one month in oncology, gastroenterology, and pathology.

When it was time to do my anesthesia rotation at St. Mary Hospital, I could not help but brag to Jim, my junior resident, that I was going to a place where the people were nicer than at Mount Sinai because they served ham sandwiches, that I missed so much, which were prohibited in a Jewish hospital!

Jim was a fitness buff who spent his free time at the gym. He tried to convince me that I should exercise by going cross-country skiing with him.

"You're asking a Haitian bush woman who spends at least thirty-six hours on a stretch going up and down the halls of Mount Sinai, to leave her cozy warm bed when she finally has some time off to rest, to put on some foolish gear and walk in the snow? You have to be crazy!"

Jim backed off pretty fast.

I hit a much harder wall with our colleague Dr. Campine, the head of anesthesia at the Wisconsin hospital. "So you want to learn to give epidural anesthesia?" he said. "Please tell me what you would do if instead of injecting the anesthesia in the epidural canal you put it in the spinal canal and paralyzed your patient; she is now unable to breathe. What will you do?"

Of course, I was speechless and didn't know the answer.

"This means you need to spend a month at Mount Sinai learning everything there is to know about anesthesia, and then you can come to St. Mary.

I was in shock, as well as disappointed, when I walked into Dr. Patel's office, the head of the anesthesia department. It was a Friday afternoon, and she was ready to leave. When I told her about my conversation with Dr. Campine, she got up and pulled out a humongous book on anesthesia, handed it to me and then looked at her schedule. Her first case on Monday was a gynecological case in OR 3, and Jim was the resident assigned to it. "Meet me there at 7 AM," she said, leaving me with that heavy book in my hands.

That whole weekend was spent cramming to learn as much as I could about anesthesia. When fitness buff Jim walked into the OR on Monday to find me at the head of the table next to Dr. Patel, he burst out laughing and made fun of me. The general surgeons and gynecologists did the same when they realized I was now the anesthesiologist. "Make sure the patient doesn't wake up in the middle of the case," they would joke.

Instead of the simple observational time I expected, I found myself working very hard. I assumed that I was going to learn how to intubate a patient and just watch the ventilators going up and down during the procedure. "Not at all," said Dr. Patel. "These machines work on electricity. Let's say that your patient is intubated, and in the middle of the procedure, there's a blackout, and the hospital generator does not work. Are you going to let your patient die? My dear, until you know how to manually ventilate your patient, you will not be using the mechanical ventilator."

I had a great learning experience with Dr. Patel. It made me more aware and sensitive as a surgeon to what an anesthesiologist does to gauge how much medication to give a patient during surgery. They must make sure the patient has enough to keep her anesthetized and pain-free during the procedure but not too much, or she would have difficulty awakening. I felt confident that if one day I had to return to Haiti or another poor country, I could be of great assistance with my additional anesthesia knowledge.

After I learned the intricate details of epidural anesthesia at St. Mary, it was time to return to Mount Sinai. One of the patients there was a dwarf woman in the high-risk obstetrics clinics, scheduled for a repeat Cesarean section with her second baby. As chief resident, I was the one who was going to handle the case, but this time not as her anesthesiologist as I had been before.

When she was admitted for her pre-op exam, she looked at me very perplexed, "Doctor, I'm confused. Are you going to put me to sleep, or are you going to deliver my baby?"

"For today," I smiled and bowed, "I will be playing the part of your obstetrician."

1981 MILWAUKEE, WISCONSIN

NO MORE SNOW FOR THE BUSH WOMAN

Straight from very warm Haiti, I had tolerated two winters in New York rather well. But while training in Milwaukee in winter, I thought my brain would freeze when I breathed. When I said how miserably cold I was, I was told to consider myself lucky because… *"You could be living in Minnesota!"*

In Milwaukee, my very first BIG snowstorm caught me by surprise. I was wearing a dress and sandals, out with a friend who was driving an older truck. It started to snow. A lot. The truck started to get stuck in the relentless snow every few blocks. Fortunately, we were on Wisconsin Avenue where there were many bars. Kind, probably liquor-warmed strangers rushed out to help get us unstuck.

Growing up in Haiti, my only knowledge of snow had been through movies or books. I remember that I was disappointed when I experienced my first snowfall in New York back in 1970. I watched out the window until the dark gray sky turned reddish and snowflakes appeared. I ran outside and threw my hands toward the sky to grab some, only to discover that those pretty snowflakes disappear immediately into drops of water when you touch them.

Now I'd had the opposite experience, with snow that stopped traffic. I decided I could live very happily without snow.

The first time I visited San Diego, it was in the middle of winter, and I was in awe that I could put my hands out the window in the middle of January and feel a warm breeze flowing through my fingers. Since I couldn't stand the freezing-cold weather of Wisconsin. I decided that Southern California was a great place to end up after my training in Milwaukee. I was going to live in San Diego, with its beautiful blue sky, warm winters, citrus fruit, palm tree and NO SNOW.

"You'll die during an earthquake," I was told, when people heard that I didn't want to stay in Milwaukee.

"If I was supposed to die in an earthquake, I could still be living here in freezing Wisconsin and get caught in one while visiting San Diego. So, this Haitian bush woman is going to enjoy the beautiful weather year-round while you continue to freeze your butts off here."

"*CHICKEN*," many would taunt, with a smirk (and maybe some envy!).

1981 MILWAUKEE, WISCONSIN

MODESTY VS CHILDBIRTH

During my residency training at Mount Sinai, I formed a strong bond with a female resident named Dhun, from India. Dhun was a devotee of Zoroastrianism, a religion and philosophy based on the teachings of the prophet Zoroaster.

Each morning we arrived at the hospital call room at 6:15 to change into the surgical scrubs we wore until it was time to go home, sometimes thirty-six hours later. Dhun and I usually entered the room at the same time, but she didn't want me there when she changed. She explained, "Modesty is one of Zoroastrianism's six virtues." Though only disrobed to our underwear, Dhun was adamant that I wait outside while she undressed.

Then Dhun got pregnant. I was the chief resident when she arrived at the hospital in labor. I chose to be her in-house doctor, and wondered how she would react to my doing her pelvic exams.

I was apprehensive when I entered her room. She was in the middle of a contraction, but still fussed to cover herself up. We talked for a while about the baby. Then the awkward moment arrived: I had to do the pelvic exam. Dhun looked at me with the wide dark eyes of a sacrificial lamb. But I performed the exam, told her my findings, and left the room.

When the time arrived, I asked her attending physician to allow me to deliver Dhun's baby. I had to perform a small episiotomy, and then the world was enriched by a beautiful, healthy baby girl named Jasmine.

The next morning when I went to see Dhun she was breast-feeding Jasmine. We both knew that checking her episiotomy site was optional, since she was experiencing no discomfort.

To my great surprise, she put Jasmine in the crib, got back in bed, and spread her legs.

"Go ahead, check me," she said with a shy smile. "After going through childbirth, I guess you can no longer be a prude."

1981 MILWAUKEE, WISCONSIN

CURSE IF YOU HAVE TO!

I n my third year of residency, I was assigned to the gyn clinic. I had been on call the night before with no chance to rest even for a few minutes. I was bone-tired and also felt like I was coming down with the flu.

After the 7 AM report, I rushed to the OR where I had to assist Dr. Castillo with an abdominal hysterectomy; and then over to assist Dr. Pearlson with a vaginal hysterectomy.

Dr. Castillo would let you do the procedure as soon as you could prove you were capable. But Dr. Pearlson only never let you do anything, he would never co-sign your notes. Most senior residents refused to scrub with him, but because he was so skilled, I felt that it was a privilege to just watch and learn from him.

Dr. Castillo guided me through the abdominal hysterectomy, which was a difficult case, and I just had the time to dictate the procedure and write the post-op notes when it was time to scrub with Dr. Pearlson.

"So, you're still scrubbing with me," he said sternly. I smiled and said I enjoyed watching and learning from him. Maybe it was my good attitude that prompted him that day to summon me over and guide me through the whole vaginal hysterectomy procedure. But he still dictated the op note and wrote his own post-op orders as usual. It was tiring, but the best day of my medical experience so far.

After these two procedures, I was too exhausted to walk over the bridge to the building where the cafeteria was located. I went straight to the call room and collapsed onto the bed. Immediately my pager went off. It was the gyn clinic. In frustration, I ignored it. Of course, I was paged again. I called Danny, my chief resident, the only one who had no other assignments, to ask if he could *please* do the clinic because it was impossible for me physically to do it.

"I'm busy," he said, while hanging up.

I was stunned. I called him back to say I was desperate. He barked, "You knew the residency program wasn't going to be a piece of cake," and hung up on me again.

I didn't know what to do. Where was I going to find the strength to continue? Maybe I was a fool; maybe I wasn't suited for this hard work? How dare I think of where I came from that I could aspire to so much and get away with it. I prayed, I summoned the spirit of Grandpa Mirabeau, Grandma, God, the voodoo spirits. Nothing worked. My pager continued to go off. Maybe it was time to quit.

Then in my despair came the image I had created during hard times… an image of me in my white coat, holding a little girl I had delivered in my private practice. I saw myself taking a picture of each of the children I would someday deliver, and covering my office walls with photos.

"No, I won't quit," I said out loud. "I've gone too far, too many sacrifices have been made; many people are praying for me and counting on me to succeed, *as a Haitian, a woman, a black woman …*"

While still in bed, I called the clinic and said I was on my way. But how could I get out of bed? I tried to, but "No way, Jose," said my battered body. I sat with tears rolling down my cheeks. I was glad to be in a windowless pit in the dark with no one looking at me.

I then forced myself to get up, went out to the labor deck and asked Mimi, the secretary, "What are the nastiest three words that you can call a man?"

Mimi was shocked, and speechless, but finally answered. "Prick, asshole, and bastard?" she offered sheepishly.

I went back to the call room and rang Danny. "What do you want?" he said angrily. "Danny, I have come so far that I'm not going to let a prick, asshole, and bastard like you stand in my way," and hung up. I didn't care about the consequences.

Then, in the small bathroom adjacent to the call room I started to scream my head off, commanding my body to get in gear and find some strength. The more I screamed and cried the stronger and better I felt. Finally, I felt strong enough to wash my face, then slowly walk to the elevator. I was on a roll. By the time I got to the clinic, I actually did well with Dr. Mintz, the medical students, and patients who had been waiting.

But I never forgot this incident. I calculated how much I was making at the time; $1.20 an hour, maybe a little more since you got free dinner when you were on call... but didn't have time to eat it.

When it was my turn to be chief resident, I changed some of the rules. I knew how hard it had been for me and I was a strong woman. The scheduling did not have to continue to be so crushingly brutal just because it was how things were done in the past.

It took many years to finally change the standard to allowing residents to work fewer hours. But in the meantime, I made sure that if a resident was on call the night before, he or she would be given something light to do the following morning, with enough time to rest and eat before attending the gyn clinics, without crying or screaming or cursing anyone out.

1981 KENOSHA, WISCONSIN

SEXISM AND RACISM

G randma had taught me to respect everyone I met, regardless of who they were. "We are all the same," she used to say, "and you have the right to expect to be treated like anyone else."

But I wasn't. I was appalled at the attitude of some of the doctors I had to work with during and after my training. Many were prejudiced, disparaging, and often blatantly racist and sexist back in the eighties. Female medical students, residents, and even patients were treated like second-class citizens by the male surgeons.

I wasn't going to be thwarted by prejudiced doctors just because I was a black woman and a foreign medical graduate. But there was no way I would work under these negative circumstances unless I did something. So, I developed a strategy: I would do what was expected of me as their "slave," using a cue card for each one describing their likes and dislikes, and then take each of them aside for a heart-to-heart talk.

My spiel was: "This is a teaching hospital. If you're so good, why don't you teach me everything there is to know? I'm here for four years, and not leaving until I'm done. I am a woman who has great things to accomplish in her life. Why don't you be part of that, and allow me to remember you forever as a great mentor instead of a jerk!" It usually worked.

I also fought for the medical students, especially the female students, to be treated with respect. I would give them a choice to wear nurse's dresses or surgical scrubs and would take those who agreed into the surgeon's lounge to get them. Of course, I made sure to knock before barging in. I didn't want the male doctors to have a heart attack.

In addition to being supportive in any way I could, at the end of the current medical students' rotation, I would treat them to a celebratory dinner at my place, serving "rice and beans and turkey en sauce,"

Haitian-style. I enjoyed sharing my heritage with so many white students.

One of those students, Lori, asked me to "walk with" her at the University of Madison as she graduated from medical school. Her uncle was a physician, but she asked me to do it because she said that I had made a big difference in her life as a medical student.

When I saw a sea of thousands of white faces graduating in that stadium in Madison, I smiled as I told Lori's family how they could easily find their daughter: "Just look for the dark face in the crowd!"

1981 MILWAUKEE, WISCONSIN

LET YOUR FINGERS DO THE "TALKING"

At that time, the city of Milwaukee welcomed a large number of Jewish refugees from Russia. They were given one year of free medical care at our hospital, Mt. Sinai.

I was more of a linguist than most of the residents – fluent in Haitian Kréyol, French, Spanish, English. But I could not speak Russian. I knew only a few words such as good morning – *dobroe utro*; good afternoon – *dobryĭ den'*; goodbye – *do svidaniya*; yes – *da*; and no – *nyet*.

One day during rounds, one of the residents was lamenting that he had a female Russian patient,

Maria, admitted for a 24-hour observation, with a history of fainting. A monitor was connected to her that would register her vital signs during activities and while resting and sleeping. When she was admitted, a Russian translator had told her that she needed to walk, in addition to resting, so the monitor could register any changes. However, she just stayed in her bed and no one knew how get her up.

"You don't need to speak someone's language to explain she needs to walk," I said to the staff. I had been called a character in the hospital, but now I could read in their eyes they suspected I'd gone off the deep end.

"You'll see; I'll have her out of bed and walking in no time." I went to the room where Maria was lying on her bed staring at the ceiling. "*Dobroe utro,*" I said with a smile as I sat on the chair next to her.

"*Dobroe utro,*" she answered with a surprised look on her face; I'm sure she had never seen a black person speaking her language. When she continued to talk in Russian, I stopped her by putting my index finger on my closed mouth. Then I put my hands over my heart gesturing somebody who was sick and going to faint.

"*Da,*" she said while nodding her head with a sad face.

I pointed at the monitor attached to her hospital gown, and placed my crossed hands back on my chest, now with a happy face. I took my index and middle fingers and made the yellow pages gesture, *"let your fingers do the walking,"* then stood up and walked back and forth in the room. I sat down, joined my two hands, placed them next to the side of my face, and closed my eyes to indicate sleep. I alternated the gestures, and she got it right away.

With a broad smile, she repeated the sequences showing she understood that she had to walk, rest, walk, rest so the monitor could find out what was wrong with her heart. This hadn't taken me five minutes to accomplish.

Maria got up, and put on a robe. I walked to the door. Like a respectful doorman, I bowed and held the door as she went by. Both of us were giggling like little girls.

When we strolled down the hall I noticed the shocked looks of the staff. You would have thought they'd seen Lazarus rising from his grave.

1982 MILWAUKEE, WISCONSIN

PAYBACK

The day before I left Milwaukee I went to Mount Sinai to say goodbye to everyone. As I walked through the hallways and stopped at each area, I could not help remembering what I had gone through the last four years, and all that I had learned in this hospital.

I was now ready to be a physician in private practice, and I knew how I was going to treat my patients.

John, one of the residents I was friendly with, decided to walk me out to my car, and we took the elevator together. The elevator was filled with residents, doctors, hospital employees and people visiting family members. Dr. Saichek, Chief of Gastroenterology, joined us on the next floor stop. I told him that it was my last day and that I was flying to San Diego the following day to start my private practice. He wished me well.

John suddenly whispered in my ear that it was too bad he never had a chance to have my long legs wrapped around his neck. Over the years, whenever we were alone, he would *always* tease and taunt me about some sexual dreams of us together, and I *always* brushed him off.

Now I had my chance to get back at him.

As the elevator door started to open on the ground floor, I quickly turned around, grabbed John's face and kissed him right on the lips. Then I ran to the parking lot.

The last picture I have of Mount Sinai framed in my mind is the shocked expression on the face of Dr. Saichek, Chief of Gastroenterology, standing behind an equally shocked John.

1989 SAN DIEGO, CALIFORNIA

PEOPLE OF COLOR

One day I was talking to a Native American friend about the importance of giving back to the community, and she suggested I volunteer my services at the Indian Urban Center in downtown San Diego. At their clinic I was able to help many of the Kumeyaay Indians whose people had been in this area for over 2000 years, but who now lived in poverty. When my own practice became so busy I couldn't put aside an entire morning at the clinic, I fit those in need into my schedule at the office.

This led to a long-term relationship with the Kumeyaay tribe, and when they started making money by building and operating casinos on their reservations, I was invited to create their first comprehensive prenatal program at the Southern Indian Health Council in Alpine, CA.

At the same time, I also became a referral gynecologist for the Salvation Army, followed by providing services at the Rachel's Women's Center, a shelter for homeless women.

In March of 1984, the El Cajon School District put together the "Women Make History Month," a collage of successful women in the community, which they distributed to every school in the district. This started my service as a role model to children of all colors and cultural backgrounds. I spoke to them about how to study hard and set goals, to never let anyone tell them they couldn't achieve their dreams, and that they were the only ones who could limit their achievements.

Soon I was being asked to speak to elementary, high school and college students, as well as the community at large. I adopted the St. Stephen Christian School, a small, black Christian school, where once a month I spoke for an hour. Our motto was: "The sky's the limit; I can be anything I want to be if I work hard for it." For another two hours I would get together with the high school students to discuss everything from self-esteem to sexual disease to career choices.

Each October the city of San Diego celebrated Women's Opportunity Week or WOW. I signed up to give a talk called "Overcoming Obstacles & Fulfilling Goals." While I was arranging where to give the talk, I was told that the keynote speaker, Mrs. Betty Ford, couldn't make it, and I was asked to take her place. "It would be great publicity for your practice, hundreds of women will learn about how you've broken through so many barriers to become a doctor." They were expecting about three hundred women at the gala. My neighbor Bill helped me write the speech and had me practice with him, with the goal of getting a standing ovation. This Haitian bush woman was honored to get one.

That standing ovation was a heart-warming balance to frequent "people of color" misconceptions I had experienced in the past...

Being a black woman wearing scrubs during my training at Mount Sinai, and wearing scrubs as a surgeon at Grossmont and Alvarado Hospitals in San Diego, I was often mistaken for a housekeeper.

I remember one day, I had a patient in long labor and had a chance to run to the cafeteria to get something to eat. A nicely-dressed woman stopped me and asked if I had found the book she left behind. I told her I was sorry that I didn't know anything about her book.

I got my food tray and started to eat, then a white male doctor I knew sat down at my table. We were chatting when the same lady came back, saw me, and looked stricken, apparently realizing her mistake. "I'm so sorry," she said, turning red as a lobster.

I smiled at her and said I didn't know what she was talking about. After she left I told my colleague what had happened, and he burst out laughing.

When I related the "housekeeper scene" to the staff in labor and delivery, we had more laughs. And from then on, whenever I went down to the cafeteria, one of them would remind me to take my bucket and broom.

1989 SAN DIEGO, CALIFORNIA

INDIGENOUS HEALING

I grew up with the understanding that healing was about more than just the body; it also involved spiritual and mental components. I was familiar with cultures where the sick used home remedies first. If that didn't work they would go to an indigenous healer, a *curandera* or a Voodoo priest or priestess, whose approach was usually a combination of conventional medical treatment and cultural healing for the removal of a hex or spell. For most people, seeking a standard medical doctor was the last resort. In Haiti, a hospital was the place people went to die.

I was fascinated by the many old rituals I encountered while caring for the sick. For example, in Haiti it was expected that for the first forty days following a baby's birth, the mother could have no sex. She must stay home for the first three days, and not shower, drink, or eat anything cold. If she had to go out, she must return by the time the sun went down.

Modern medical practice had some established rituals of its own that made little apparent sense, which I abolished from my own practices. For example, I eliminated the mandatory "prep and shave" part of the childbirth process, where the hair on top of the patient's pubic bone and the vulva – the labia and the opening of the vagina – were shaved, and getting an enema.

As a resident, I could never stand seeing these poor women in labor running back and forth to the bathroom. I was one of the few doctors who let mothers not suffering from complications do whatever they wanted in the delivery room, such as being free to walk around instead of being strapped to a monitor. I also allowed them to have as many visitors as they wanted during labor, instead of the rigid number of two. Why not? While I was working in the Pueblos, the family dog often joined us!

I did my best to stay with a mother while she was pushing. Too often a C-section would be considered when the mother began tiring, but my staying and encouraging her to push could re-invigorate her. I would wipe her sweaty forehead with a washcloth and join her in screaming at the father-to-be that it was "your fault I'm going through all this hell." Thank God for epidurals.

While the mother was pushing I would thin out her perineum to decrease the likelihood of an episiotomy, just I had watched my mother, the indigenous mid-wife, do when I was eleven, during one of my rare visits with her. I also did not mind doing the delivery in the bed if the patient didn't want to use stirrups.

Whenever I was in the labor room I made everyone laugh. While helping a mother push I would say that my hemorrhoids were going to pop since I was involuntarily pushing as well. When the baby came out squirming, I would hold it in my arms and present it to the family, saying "this is one of the most beautiful babies I have ever seen." And it always was.

If a C-section had to be done, I would write, "Diet as tolerated" in my post-op notes instead of starting the patient on clear liquids. Any sane person would eat only when they were able to, anyway.

I followed no medical postpartum traditions except for reminding patients they should bring their babies back for a six-week checkup, at which time I would take a picture to adorn my ever-growing photo wall of lovely babies that I had delivered.

Before long I was known as the doctor who took a holistic (indigenous-informed) approach to caring for patients, including believing that patients had the right to accept or refuse care.

1990 SAN DIEGO, CALIFORNIA

NO, YOU CAN'T BE THE SURGEON!

It was interesting when a local committee decided they were going to depict the lives of black folks in San Diego in a photo display. I was one of those chosen as I had been in the news before for receiving various awards, as a medical expert on women's health, my volunteer work, or interviewed each time there was turmoil in Haiti.

The photographer assigned to me requested to be in the delivery room to take pictures of the birth of a black baby, with the mother's permission – and of course standing at the head of the bed and not looking at the poor woman's crotch. It wasn't easy to arrange since only about one in ten patients was black, and having one deliver during the timing of the photo shoot was asking for a miracle. But we were lucky and photos were taken successfully.

The photo exhibit took place at the Lyceum Theatre in the new Horton Plaza in downtown San Diego. It was with happy anticipation that my friend Shirley and I looked through all the San Diego Union Tribune pictures to find mine. There I was in my scrubs and surgical mask, holding a beautiful little black infant boy, and of course, posing like a model.

Unfortunately, the caption on my photo was, *"Nurse who helped deliver the baby."*

I was not pleased to be overlooked as the obstetrician. My staff, friends, and many patients were adamant that I call the newspaper, demand an apology, and even consider suing for discrimination. When I called and introduced myself, I received a verbal apology and was told that the phone had been ringing off the hook with infuriated people saying that mistake would have never been made if it was a white male holding the baby.

Two days later, buried in the back of the paper, was a short statement in tiny type correcting the error identifying me.

I kept a copy of the lovely photo from the exhibit, pasted the correction I cut out of the newspaper over that mistaken caption, and racked it up as another ironic day in the life of a female surgeon.

1991 SAN DIEGO, CALIFORNIA

THE BELLY DANCING GYNECOLOGIST

During my last year of residency at Mount Sinai, I wanted to find a different hobby, something relaxing and fun that I could do all year round. And then I was introduced to belly dancing.

While going through our grueling medical training, we would find time to go to parties given by the other residents, mostly disco dancing. We even had a toga party once. I'm sure the hospital was very short of linen that night!

Bonnie, one of the intensive care unit nurses, was a great dancer to watch at these parties because she had great rhythm. She was small-framed, about

5'4" with beautiful long auburn hair, a gorgeous smile, and dark blue eyes. My boyfriend and I would be the only black couple at those parties – and we knew how to move to the beat of the Pointer Sisters, the Bee Gees, and, of course, Donna Summer. But Bonnie was the life of the parties with her dancing skill.

One day, Bonnie invited me to go with her to a belly dancing show featuring dancers from all over the world. I ran to Bonnie after the first intermission and said: "I now know why you dance so well; you're a belly dancer!"

She was happy to introduce me to her teacher, Atea, who gave me her business card in case I might be interested in taking classes. I was definitely interested, and Bonnie promised that we could practice together.

I convinced one of my friends, Linea, who I had befriended during my rotation in anesthesia, to take classes with me. We signed up for the eight-week class for beginners. They took place in a ballet studio with huge mirrors on the wall. After stretching, we would proceed to learn the different, and intricate, arm, hip, shoulder, leg, and pelvic movements. It was awkward at first, but soon I was really into the movements. I knew I'd found my new hobby.

I bought a belt made of steel rings and coins that was somewhat heavy but actually helped you to hear your hip movements. We wore leotards at first; then either had to learn to make simple costumes with large scarves, skirts, or harem pants, or purchase one already made through a catalog. Atea told me that it would be more fun to make it myself. Good idea, as I wasn't sure there were any belly dancing costumes readily available for a six-foot-tall women like me.

My sewing lessons with Grandma in Haiti when I was young– something that I had to do *or else* – came in handy again. Of course, I had to find time in my busy schedule to design and sew. My goal was to have a costume ready and to learn enough steps to have a two-song dance show in six weeks. Linea, who had quit because she felt she didn't have the rhythm for it, helped with my costume, and Bonnie helped me with the choreography.

The costume consisted of a shear silk fabric from a very colorful old Indian sari. I cut it into three parts: one small piece for a headscarf, another rectangular piece about five feet long for a veil, and the rest to make a hip to ankle-length skirt. The back was one large panel, but the front had three openings at mid-thigh level. I went to a fabric store for silver sequins, and transformed a regular bra into a sexy top.

It was so much fun learning how to belly dance, and to create my own costume. It was daring; I was a doctor in a conservative town and hospital who would be in public in a sequined bra and see-though veils. I was already being called a character... but who had ever heard of a belly dancing resident surgeon?

The nurses, the other residents, and the medical students were having fun with my new hobby as well. We would go into an empty patient room so I could teach them some movements. They especially loved the belly rolls.

"So, I heard you're becoming a belly dancer," was the comment I would get from the attending physicians. "You'll develop some nice pyramidalis muscles."

One morning I got to the hospital conference room for the 7 AM report and saw everyone looking at me with excitement. I was asked: "Did you watch the TV show *That's Incredible* last night? There was a belly dancer who knelt down with her back almost touching the floor, and rolled a series of four quarters, one at a time, and together, up and down her abdomen!"

No, I hadn't seen it. The only show I watched in my spare time was *Quincy*, a TV series about a pathologist who resolved rare medical cases. But I happily agreed to try rolling quarters on my belly when I got home that night, and tell them the results the next morning.

That evening I assumed the dancer's position and put four quarters on my abdomen. No matter how hard I tried, I could not make them roll over. They would move a little or just slide off. It was really difficult to micro-manage those specific muscles. No wonder she had made it onto *That's Incredible*!

The next morning I mischievously kept the students and residents in suspense until we got together for the morning report. "Sorry," I told shook my head sadly, "I couldn't move one quarter, no less four of them." They were disappointed but agreed it must take years of practice to master that trick.

Around this time, when I was asked to contribute as chief resident to the department newsletter, I proposed writing an article about the benefits of belly dancing. When the newsletter came out, on one page was the announcement: "*Dr. Carolle Jean-Murat has been accepted as a Junior Fellow of the American College of Obstetrics and Gynecology.*"

Ironically on the next page of the newsletter was my article: "Tired of running, jogging, and dieting, try a spectator sport: *Belly Dancing*," featuring a picture of Bonnie and me in our sexy belly dancer costumes. I never heard the end of it at the hospital.

When Bonnie came to visit, she fell in love with San Diego and eventually made it her home. So did Atea, our teacher, who one day called me about an idea of doing a belly dancing video, the first of its kind.

She wanted me to be part of *Atea and Friends Belly Dancing Video.*

"Let me think about it," I said. I thought if I was going to formally proclaim myself as a belly dancer, I would need to choose a stage name. "Yes, I'll do it," I told a delighted Atea. And so "Akisha," after my niece Kisha, was born.

The date was set for the studio taping and we had to practice a lot beforehand. Practicing and taping that belly dancing video was quite a memorable event in my life. The video turned out great.

While I was putting together a set of costumes and practicing for it, I was also assembling the cases required to take my oral board in Chicago. A while after I took the exam, a letter came congratulating me on passing the board, and soon I would apply to become a Fellow of the American College of Obstetricians and Gynecologists. I would then *officially* be known as Carolle Jean-Murat, MD, FACOG, Belly Dancer!

Some years later I received an unexpected call from the TV show *Entertainment Tonight.* They had seen Atea's video, were doing a show about the beneficial effects of belly dancing, and wanted to interview me, the belly dancing doctor!

I was so excited; I couldn't have known that this video, made years ago, would land me a spot on

national television. Belly dancing had been beneficial to me as exercise and a way to de-stress, as well
as showing my mischievous side.

I sent a message to John Tesh, the show's host,
about how to pronounce my name correctly. My seg-
ment was featured between clips about Liza Minnelli,
and Randy Travis. My friends asked how John Tesh
got my name right. I laughed and said, "Because he
was warned he'd be in deep trouble if he mispro-
nounced it on my national TV debut!"

That day, in the gossip column in the San Diego
Union Tribune, Tom Blair wrote: "*San Diego Seen:
Today Dr. Carolle Jean-Murat's patients will have the op-
portunity to see her belly button on ET.*"

1991 SAN DIEGO, CALIFORNIA

WHO'S HARASSING WHO?

G rossmont Hospital had never had a woman ob-gyn surgeon when I joined the staff, and I remained the only one for the next four years. The labor and delivery area had two small sleeping rooms plus a doctor's lounge with nice lockers for the male doctors. Whenever I had a delivery scheduled, I would quickly use one of the rooms to change, pushing my purse and clothes under the bed because I had no locker.

During some cases, I would find myself waiting in this lounge, where all the scrubs were located. At first, when a male doctor wanted to change, I would leave the room. When that got old I decided that if a fellow surgeon was too uncomfortable to change in my presence, he should be the one to leave. I teased them by saying, "You have nothing I haven't seen before!"

The situation was slightly different in the main operating room. The only other female surgeon was Dr. Maria Castillejos, a Mexican-born ophthalmologist with a petite frame who fit perfectly in the nurses' quaint little dresses. I was a six-foot-tall large-framed woman who was comfortable wearing large scrubs, and was not ready to wear any sissy dresses just to conform to the status quo. They wouldn't fit me anyway. It meant that I had to come in earlier to deal with scrubs, and add another five minutes to be with my patient before they put her to sleep. It was important to me that she had someone to comfort her while she was being put to sleep and not be surrounded by complete strangers.

If I had to do a gynecological procedure, since there were no empty lockers in the nurses' changing room, I was expected to put my clothes on a bench and give my purse to the head nurse for safekeeping. One day, my case was delayed, and when I went back to the office I couldn't find the head nurse to retrieve my purse. I asked to be taken to the operating room doctor's lounge to wait.

What a shock. It was a huge lounge with sofas, a small refrigerator with juices, snacks, and fruits. In the early mornings, there were freshly-baked muffins, and during lunchtime, a variety of sandwiches. The changing area was very spacious, with empty lockers open and keys attached. Wow. After taking my clothes off and putting on my scrubs, I could just put my clothes and my purse inside the locker, lock it, place the key in my pocket and go do my surgery. When my case was over, I could quickly change and waste no time. I also found out that I could use my key to the doctor's parking lot to get access to that lounge. When I got to my office, I called the head of the surgery and the ob-gyn department to let them know that I had decided from now on to change in the doctor's lounge.

The next time I had a surgery, I walked into the changing room where the men were in all stages of undressing. Everyone froze. It was like they had turned back to look at Sodom and Gomorrah and turned into salt. I said good morning, proceeded to get my scrubs, use a shower stall to change, put my clothes in the locker and my key in my pocket and said, "See you." Nobody had moved.

A few days later, I got a call from the assistant to the hospital administrator, asking me for a truce. I told her that I was one of their best surgeons, and that since most of my patients had very good insurance, the hospital needed me. I did not need them because I could go to any other hospital, but I was not planning to move. I told him that I would stop changing in the doctor's dressing room if I were provided an adequate space to change, anywhere. So, they constructed a special locker in the nurse's changing room, and I was promised an adequate supply of large doctor's scrubs.

Whenever a new doctor joined the hospital staff, he was jokingly told to *be careful of Dr. Jean-Murat, the woman doctor harassing the poor male doctors.*

I won't deny it.

Once I had an emergency Cesarean, and there were no scrubs in the area where they had put aside a call room for female doctors to put on surgical attire. Fed up, I just walked across the hall into the spacious doctor's lounge. There was Dr. Maguire giving a tour to Dr. Nguyen, who had just joined the staff. I guess they were talking about me when I showed up. Poor Dr. Nguyen was in his underwear and looking at me in a state of shock.

"There she is, the crazy woman I told you about," said Dr. Maguire.

"Nice to meet you," I said to Dr. Nguyen, taking some scrubs and leaving with a grin.

During the Anita Hill and Clarence Thomas controversy about sexual harassment, I was asked to do a television interview, since I was one of the few women physicians on staff at my hospital. They asked if I ever had to deal with harassment.

I could not stop laughing.

I finally replied, "Actually, it's the other way around. I was the one harassing those poor guys; maybe one of them should be interviewed."

1991 SAN DIEGO, CALIFORNIA

I'LL DELIVER IN MY UNDERWEAR!

Grossmont Hospital invested over $25 million into a women's center with all the labor rooms being **LDRP** (Labor Delivery Recovery Postpartum) suites. It took five years to build the center, which opened in 1990. I was only interested in one thing: a female doctors' locker room with a shower, scrubs, hats, shoe covers, and masks, just as in the male doctors' locker room.

We now had three female ob-gyns on staff. Nevertheless, a new architect took over at the last minute and slashed plans for the women physicians' locker room.

We were told we would have to change in the nurses' locker room, which consisted of a row of lockers and two benches, with no place to shower. In the end, because we demanded to have a place of our own, they took the bed out of one of the small sleeping rooms and put three lockers against the wall. There they placed a chair, a bin for dirty scrubs, and enough room for a small cabinet with a few clean scrubs.

Whenever I was called to the hospital for an emergency, there was always something missing in that make-shift locker room; no scrubs, no hat, no mask, or no shoe covers. I was infuriated by the whole thing, especially since I was expected at any time of the day or night, to perform at 120 percent, yet the support I got never went above 75 percent. I realized that if I were taking care of my patients the same way, there would be many incident reports written against me, and I would be asked to resign from the hospital staff.

Whenever I complained about the inefficient situation, I got the same stock response, "Sorry, Dr. Jean Murat, we'll try our best the next time."

I lost my temper finally one day when called to the hospital for an emergency delivery. Arriving to hurriedly change my clothes, I found NO scrub pants in "our" locker room.

So, I called the desk in charge and stated, "If I don't get a pair of scrub pants in sixty seconds, I'll go deliver my patient's baby in my underwear."

1991 DETROIT, MICHIGAN

THERE IS CLASS IN DETROIT

I had to attend an advanced laparoscopy class in Chicago in October, and decided that I would to take a side trip and visit Marie Carmelle, a childhood friend and her family. She was living in Toronto, with her husband Ed, working as a translator and mediator, and three children. I was invited and told that I would have my own room, that there were no cats or dogs, and that no one smoked or burned incense – pre-requisites for me to stay overnight in anyone's home.

It was a beautiful Indian summer, and Ed promised to take us on many outings, including going to see the Canadian side of Niagara Falls in all its splendor. Then, before I'd fly back to San Diego, he'd drive all of us across the border to visit a mutual friend, Frantzie, down in Detroit.

"*Detroit*! What's there to see or do in Detroit?" my friends and patients exclaimed when they heard about my itinerary. I said I'd get back to them about that.

After my medical class, I flew Air Canada from Chicago into Toronto. It was a breathtaking panorama seeing the colorful trees in early fall. I loved Toronto, a metropolitan area with beautiful buses that took you everywhere. Marie Carmelle and I had the opportunity to spend time alone reminiscing about our childhood and Grandma. We listened to the tape she had made and could not help laughing hysterically. Grandma was very humorous and a great storyteller.

We had many lovely outings in Toronto, then Ed drove us down to Detroit to visit Frantzie. I didn't know what to expect.

I was pleasantly surprised when Frantzie took the time to show us many different areas of interest in Detroit, such as the Renaissance Center, a group of seven interconnected skyscrapers, and much, much more. We even had dinner in a fancy Italian restaurant that featured an opera singer.

Now I knew first-hand that I could go back to San Diego and say that yes, they do have class in Detroit.

1994 SAN DIEGO, CALIFORNIA

TOUGH LOVE!

I do not smoke and never did. It was not the thing for a girl to do when I was growing up in Haiti. When patients talk about nicotine cravings, I can only relate it to food cravings.

Whenever we have a small earthquake in California, I always fear that I could be stuck in a place where there's no food. My worst nightmare is being abandoned on a small island with one fruit-less palm tree and no drinkable water. My family, my friends, and my staff know the Haitian bush woman has to eat when she's hungry. Sometimes I'm ashamed of times when I have found myself in some corner of the world stopping for fast food, just because of uncontrollable cravings. And so, I do understand the concept of craving something physically, emotionally, and mentally.

I also empathize with those affected by second-hand smoke. I have had environmental allergies since I was a child. Being exposed to any air pollution makes me ill. It usually starts with an itchy nose, then difficulty breathing, and, if I remain in the area, an acute headache.

Living in California where anti-smoking sentiments are high has been a blessing for my health. Since the only close contact I now have with smokers is with some of my patients, my sensitivity to cigarette smoke is getting *worse…* but this helps my patients because I give them "tough love."

I've found that one incentive for a woman to quit smoking is the simple fact that her healthcare provider emphasizes it at each visit. An article in the newsletter of the American College of Obstetrics and Gynecology, of which I am a fellow, stressed that the practitioner should make sure to discuss smoking cessation with each smoker and during each visit. This article, along with my allergies, has prompted me to scold my patients without mercy!

I don't have to read the health questionnaire of a new patient or hear from her that she hasn't quit smoking to know if she smokes. I just have to be in a closed room with her! I have always told patients rather bluntly that they "stink," and because of my allergies, their visit would have to be limited to their current complaint. So, unfortunately, patients who smoke cannot linger to chat with me, which I always like to do when time permits.

My patients who smoke are told that they're inconsiderate because they come to see me so that they will experience better health, and in the process, they're making me sick! They promise to quit before their next appointment, and we agree on a date to quit before they leave my office.

Some of my colleagues cannot believe that I do this to my patients. It may seem rude to some, but this approach seems to work. It is a personal triumph when I have a patient who has been smoking for years tell me that she finally quit because she was tired of hearing me tell her about the "stink."

Should I stop telling patients to quit smoking? The patients themselves urge me to continue this practice of "tough love." So, patients who are smokers, watch out!

1994 SAN DIEGO, CALIFORNIA

THE DREADED GYNECOLOGICAL EXAM

I 'm not sure which I dislike most, going to the gynecologist or going to the dentist. Though I'm a gynecologist myself, when I'm on that table, underneath that paper gown, I am a patient like everyone else. The actress Cher, while playing a gynecologist in a movie, said, "You are never too rich, never too young, and never too far from the end of the table."

Just like every other patient, I must work up the courage to call for an appointment with my gynecologist. I have sometimes been able to delay this dreaded encounter for weeks at a time. But eventually, the reality of the visit approaches like doom.

It starts the night before when I look at the calendar and realize, "Tomorrow is THE day."

When I wake up in the morning the discomfort sets in. What am I going to wear? Where is my best underwear? What about my shoes? My feet sweat and my shoes don't always smell so great, so I choose new shoes or shoes that have been waiting for months at the back of my closet for a special occasion. I have to find a brand-new pair of pantyhose. While I'm getting dressed, I look at the crop of hair in my armpits. Should I shave? I grew up in a culture where shaving was not part of a woman's body ritual. Will I feel self-conscious if I don't? Are my toenails clean enough? They're going to be hanging out on either side of the doctor's face.

By the time I'm in the car, I'm hoping that I'll be paged to an emergency so I can delay the inevitable again. And I can't even think about the possibility that something might turn up in the exam, especially because, as a gynecologist, I know all the things that can go wrong.

When I finally arrive, I remind the nurse taking my blood pressure and weight that I hate the whole thing. "Do you have to weigh me? I'm sure that I've regained all of the pounds I lost last year." "Yes, I do," she tells me sweetly.

My gynecologist, Dr. Myelin Ho, knows that I hate to sit dressed in those embarrassing paper gowns, so she rarely makes me wait. "There you are, finally," she'll say with her warm smile. "Let's do it and get it over with," I reply.

While I'm stretched out on the hard, cold examining table, she tries to talk to me while her gentle hands are examining my body. Looking up, I laugh as I remember that in one office I've had, I placed signs on the ceiling to be read while you're lying on the table. One said, *"Don't worry; nobody is perfect, except you."* Another one said, *"Patience is a virtue, even in a situation like this."* And the last one, my patients' favorite, *"Stop complaining, I have to go through it too!"*

I feel tense. "Go limp," I repeat to myself, while trying to disappear from the face of the earth. "It's over," my doctor finally says. "You're in perfect condition."

I remember what Grandma used to say to me, "Everything comes to an end." Even so, as soon as Dr. Ho leaves the room, I jump off the table, throw on my clothes, and run out that door!

1994 SAN DIEGO, CALIFORNIA

THE SKY'S THE LIMIT

B efore I started traveling back to Haiti to do volunteer work in 1999, I spent time with some special children in the San Diego community. I "adopted" the St. Stephen's Christian School of mostly black children K1-12, led by Bishop George McKinney and his wife. I fell in love with the children in their school uniforms. When I looked at their bright faces, I saw myself in every one of them.

Once a month, I would spend a whole morning at the school. We gathered first for an hour in the church so all the grades could fit in, and we would start with one student coming in front of the class to recite something I taught them: *"The sky's the limit. I can be anything that I want to be if I work hard for it."* All the children would repeat it proudly. Then we would discuss a motivating topic. The rest of the morning I spent with grades nine through twelve to answer questions about a chosen topic or to talk about anything they wanted to address.

Now, years later, it gives me such a good feeling when a young lady or gentleman unexpectedly approaches me in the supermarket or somewhere else and with a big smile says, *"The sky's the limit. I can be anything that I want to be if I work hard for it."*

They tell me that they had never forgotten the mantra, and that because they took it to heart, they are doing well in life. Many of these children, now in college, or in postgraduate school, have parents who never graduated from high school.

What a profound influence we can have on self-esteem with positive motivation. Because of my own experience, I told these children they should "dare to dream big." That the only barriers they could not overcome were those they placed in front of themselves. That it would not matter whether they were black, or female, as long as words like honesty, integrity, character, goals and hard work were part of their vocabulary. That they should never settle for anything small. That they should buck the status quo, ignore prejudice, and keep motivating themselves.

And that they could be doctors, lawyers, teachers, president of this country. The sky's the limit!

I specifically told those children that they should never worry about statistics or people who say to those who dare dream big that "it's impossible to do something because no one else like them had ever done such a thing." I told them about my own story – that in Haiti when I decided to become a doctor, I had never seen a woman doctor before. That when I decided to come to San Diego because I loved the weather, I was told that I could never make it because people were prejudiced and I could never have a successful practice as a black woman doctor. And the list of negatives would go on and on!

A while back, I was talking to Durélène, a lovely sixteen-year-old girl who I'd invited to spend the weekends with me. She was born in Haiti, her parents and her many siblings came to this country as refugees when she was nine, and they all lived a modest life. I promised that she could spend as much time as she wanted with me. I would offer the refuge I wished I had when I was her age and felt that I belonged nowhere. I call her "my weekend daughter."

The first time we spent the weekend together, we were talking about her dreams, and she told me that she wanted to be a lawyer, but feared she may not be able to make it because she's a woman and she's black.

My answer to her was that the only thing she could not be in this country was the president. And NOT because she is a woman or black, but only because in the US constitution a foreign-born person cannot run for president. It made my heart happy to see the light of hope in her eyes.

1995 LONG ISLAND, NEW YORK

LITTLE RASCALS

I was in New York visiting my brother Lesly's house, and the second night I was there someone was needed to babysit my two nieces and three nephews, ranging in age from three to eleven. They were in the habit of running up and down the stairs from the basement to the second floor, screaming all the way.

Somehow, I got the babysitting job. A few minutes after everyone left, to stop the noise, I decided to have a talk with the "Little Rascals." I had them line up in front of me and then asked if they knew why Tattie (Auntie) Carolle did not have any kids.

By the blank way they looked at me I realized they had no idea whether I had children

So, looking at each one straight in the eyes, I said that I used to have five kids their age, but when I got tired of their noise… they just "disappeared." They were shocked silent.

I continued in a pleasant tone saying that if they wanted their mother and father to be able to find them in the house when they returned, they had to behave, find a corner to read something, watch TV, draw, or fall asleep, and leave Tattie Carolle in peace. If they wanted something to eat or drink, or needed help they could ask politely.

They scattered.

In a short while, Rita Robotham, a dear friend from Montego Bay who lived in NY, came by to see me and reminisce about the good old days in Jamaica.

"You're all by yourself tonight," she said.

"Nope, I'm babysitting two nieces and three nephews under the age of eleven."

She thought I was joking because the house was so quiet, so we went around looking for the rascals. When we found them all sleeping in the basement, we tip-toed out.

Upstairs, I told Rita what I had said to them, and we couldn't stop laughing.

I worried a little that I might have traumatized the Little Rascals.

Years later I asked them if they remembered that night, but to my relief, none of them did. They just knew Tattie Carolle did not like noise, but she loved them. And so I stopped feeling guilty that I might have had anything to do with any of them ever being screwed up.

1995 SAN DIEGO, CALIFORNIA

MYRNA'S NIPPLE PIERCINGS

I got a big surprise while examining my patient Myrna during her yearly checkup. She had both of her nipples pierced.

Ouch!!! This was the first nipple piercing I had seen, and I was in shock. I could not imagine experiencing the pain to do such a thing. Myrna was just as surprised to see my reaction, and we had a good laugh together. She told me that she figured as a gynecologist who spent her days examining women's breasts, I would have seen pierced nipples before. I had seen many body piercings over the years, but not this type. Any time I saw a body piercing, I would experience a weird feeling, like someone scratching a blackboard.

Myrna pulled down her paper top so I could do the breast exam. She had a gold ring the size of a ring finger going right through the middle of each nipple. Each one had a small red bead hanging on the ring.

"Was it painful?" I asked, while examining them. There was no infection or bad scarring. The rings moved very freely under my fingers, and Myrna's face did not signal that I was making her uncomfortable.

"No, it wasn't painful the first time," she said. "The second time, yes."

"Twice? What are you talking about?" I asked her. She proceeded to explain that the first time she'd had them pierced, the guy inserted silver rings. Later she decided that she didn't like the silver ones, and went to another guy to have them switched to gold rings. Only the guy who did it the first time had used ice to freeze the nipples so it wouldn't hurt.

I couldn't imagine someone freezing my nipples, or even touching me with cold hands. Myrna was laughing at the horror on my face. "By the way," she added, "both guys have a very good reputation around town for using sterile instruments," as if that would comfort me.

"What made you want to do this?" I asked.

"I just wanted to do something daring for the first time in my life. A friend of mine had one nipple done, and when I heard about it, I was shocked by the idea. But the more I thought about it, the more I wanted to do it. And when I decided to do it, I chose to go for both nipples. I talked to my husband about it beforehand. He said that I was too young to be going through a midlife crisis, but that it was my body, my choice. So, I went ahead, and I'm glad I did. For the first time in my life, the little girl who was raised to be prim and proper has done something daring."

Since Myrna was grinning about this accomplishment, I smiled back and said, "I totally understand the part about doing something *daring*, but that's as far as I can go on this subject."

1997 SAN DIEGO, CALIFORNIA

WEIGHING IN ON WEIGHT

It's probably ironic that I occasionally find myself trying to lose weight like everyone else these days. I grew up in a culture where being plump was equated with wealth and health. Women, who could afford it, actually injected themselves with "Durabolin," an expensive steroid, to maintain plumpness.

I remember my teenage years, being self-conscious about my lanky body. Not only did I have to deal with being very tall, but I was also very skinny. My little brother, Lesly, used to call me Gran' Pélé, a witch character in our stories who dressed in all black and flew on a broomstick. When I was seventeen, my cousin, Marie José, sent me a pair of blue jeans from Canada, where she was attending college. It was not customary for girls to wear pants at that time in Haiti. The first and last time I wore those tight jeans, people on the street looked at me as if I were some kind of freak. One man even asked if my parents had enough food to feed me!

While I was in medical school, my roommate Nicole and I decided that we needed to gain some weight. Nicole was not as tall as I was, but she was obsessed with her belly being too flat. We would save our money and buy fattening food at the cafeteria. Nicole would lift up her blouse for me to inspect her belly to see if it was getting any plumper. I used to laugh at her and tell her to eat even more.

Today, Nicole is married to another Haitian, Fanell, and has two children, Philip, my godson, and Michele. The years have gone by and now we are both watching our weight. Nicole complains that her belly is too big and she wants to lose it. She is as concerned now about losing weight as she once was about gaining it.

Here in the US, we constantly live with guilt about eating. Most of us are on some kind of diet. What good is it to be able to afford to buy whatever we want when we're restricted because we're trying to lose weight? Which is worse: not having enough money to buy food and going hungry, or having all the food we want and sometimes starving ourselves to be thin?

Once in my thirties, after I had gained some extra weight, I worked very hard to lose it. I loved how I felt and looked in the mirror, proud to wear my good clothes again. I remember the first day I was able to wear a beautiful red pantsuit with white trim and gold buttons that Mother had sent me for motivation. I promised myself that I would never gain back that weight!

When that red pantsuit began getting too tight, it was a wake-up call! How had that weight so mysteriously returned?

Well, it wasn't a mystery…The previous weekend I had worked very long hours. At the hospital all night and all morning, two days before my period started, I was cranky and hungry. In the hospital cafeteria, the food looked tasteless. I reluctantly took a piece of chicken and some vegetables. When I got to the cashier, however, I noticed some heart-shaped chocolate candies. I could not control myself! I grabbed as many as I could fit in my hand, and started to eat one before I paid the cashier.

"Dr. Jean-Murat, I can see that you're hooked on chocolate," she said with a smile. I answered her with a grin, busy chewing, then hurried to the corner of the cafeteria, far away from everybody. I did not dare go to the doctor's lounge as I would have been ashamed to be seen.

By the time I had finished the tasteless chicken, I had already eaten four more of the chocolates. I ate two more on the way to my car. Guilt crept over me. I'll save the last one for tomorrow, I promised myself.

When I got home I really wanted to eat that last chocolate. My guilt level was very high, but for some reason I didn't care. So I reached for it. It was a hot day, and when I tried to unwrap the piece, it had melted and was stuck to the foil. I didn't want to lose any of it, so I put it in the freezer and anxiously checked on it until, after an eternity, the foil could be peeled off. I almost swallowed it whole.

Guilt crushed down on me.

"I'll exercise a lot tomorrow," I said to the empty foil wrapper, thinking wistfully of my red pantsuit.

1997 SAN DIEGO, CALIFORNIA

IS IT MY GENES OR IS IT MENOPAUSE?

Katherine, a fifty-two-year-old patient of mine, came to my office because she was experiencing many menopause-related symptoms. Apparently, while seated in the waiting room, she had a conversation with another patient regarding her symptoms. She couldn't help noticing the facial hair on the woman she was speaking to. That woman said she had been menopausal for three years and was on hormone replacement therapy.

Katherine's first frantic words to me were: "Dr. Jean-Murat, am I going to grow hair on my face like the other patient?" I explained to her that the previous patient had excessive facial hair completely unrelated to menopause.

She was so relieved to learn that women do not start growing beards because of menopause!

I filled her in a little more about menopause: "Throughout a woman's adult life, her ovaries do produce some testosterone, the male hormone. During menopause, the production of testosterone is reduced by two-thirds, but since the production of estrogen becomes minimal, the body produces relatively more testosterone. This explains why some women display signs of masculinization, like a deeper voice or increased hairiness. There can also be a thinning of hair.

As you age, your skin will change somewhat, but again it hasn't been proven that menopause is the direct cause. The skin grows thinner and loses its elasticity, resulting in wrinkling. Some of this is due to a reduction in the skin's collagen content. Black women have fewer wrinkles because of the abundance of melanin and the thickness of their skin. (I call it a blessing.) But wrinkles are not an inevitable part of aging! People exposed to the sun are much more prone to premature aging of the skin. Fair-skinned people are more vulnerable to wrinkles."

I told her that aging of the skin depends on race and genes. In my family, the older we get, the younger we look. I tell my envious white patients and friends that we are like fine wine: the older, the better.

I had never paid much attention to wrinkles until one day when Grandma and I were shopping, she asked me to buy her a jar of Noxzema. I asked why she needed it. She had been watching television and had seen a Noxzema commercial featuring a beautiful woman with smooth skin. I was a little perplexed since Grandma spoke no English and never wore make-up, but had somehow become convinced that Noxzema would help her get rid of her wrinkles. I took a good look at Grandma's smooth eighty-year-old face; what she had noticed were a few natural laugh lines. Grandma's beautiful face had no wrinkles. "Are you getting vain in your old age?" I asked her. "You don't need any cream; you were born smiling with these lines."

Recently, I was invited to be a guest speaker for a group of professional black women. The rather serious discussion centered on the difficulties involved in our daily lives.

Before we concluded, I wanted them to understand that, in spite of the trials and tribulations they encountered daily, they had a *precious gift*.

They looked intrigued.

I told them this little story: One day, God came to earth to visit a group of black women. "I know what you are going through," God said. "Others often place you at the bottom of the totem pole. To make up for this, I am going to bestow a great gift upon you. It is the gift of ever-lasting beauty. While others grow old like prunes, your skin will always be youthful. You will be the envy of all the races. You will not have to spend your hard-earned money on wrinkle creams or plastic surgery."

The ladies gave that story a standing, laughing, ovation!

1997: SAN DIEGO, CALIFORNIA

TOO MUCH SEX

An estimated thirty million American men over the age of sixty suffer from impotence, the difficulty in obtaining or maintaining an erection. Impotence can be associated with illnesses like diabetes or depression. Treatments for impotence have included injections into the penis, suppositories, implants, or vacuum devices that cause the penis to fill with blood.

With Viagra, Cialis, and other medications for male impotence, we have a phenomenon that has taken the sexual world by storm. Men used to lie about how often they were *having* sex; now they exaggerate how they *can't* have sex because of impotence… in order to get the prescription!

When men rushed to get this miracle drug, I saw the effects in my office. Women, who for years had to repress their sexuality because of their mate's inability to perform, were now having fulfilling sexual relationships. But some of them were having great difficulty coping with this renewed sexual vigor.

One such woman was Laura, seventy years old, with a seventy-seven-year-old husband who started taking Viagra. When they came to my office, the husband did most of the talking. I guessed something was going on because Laura barely spoke, so, I asked him to leave during Laura's examination. She started to cry the minute he left.

"Dr. Carolle, I feel like a sex slave and a prisoner to this stranger who used to be my husband! There's no place to run or hide in the confinement of the mobile home we live in. He wants sex all the time! I'm sore; I don't want it; I want out. But I do love this man, the father of my children. I'm desperate and just don't know what to do."

Laura also expressed fear that her attitude might cause her husband to look outside their marriage for sex, which she would not be able to tolerate.

A horrifying scene came to mind…. the Lorena Bobbit case. (For those who are not familiar, Lorena allegedly had an abusive husband. One night, she cut off her husband's penis with a kitchen knife, then drove off, and threw it in a field. The penis had to be retrieved and surgically re-attached.)

As a concerned physician, I had to find an alternative for Laura's distress. So, I started her on testosterone cream, at the lowest dose, which she could apply daily to her inner thigh.

It either worked to increase her libido, or had a placebo effect, because two months later, I received a phone call from a contented husband requesting a refill!

1998 SAN DIEGO, CALIFORNIA

ME AND MY BREASTS

My relationship with my breasts started on the wrong foot.

I was a tomboy born in Haiti of a 5 '8" father and a 4' 9" mother. For whatever reasons, I was destined to be six feet tall in a country where the average woman was about 5' 2".

I was the first-born. My younger sister Marise, who reached 5' 4", had breasts by age ten and was menstruating by age twelve. Like everything else that I do in my life, I had to be different. While my little sister was becoming a woman in front of my eyes, I was growing taller and taller, with no sign of puberty.

The male doctor took a look at my naked, lanky body and decided that nothing was wrong with me: I was just going through a growth spurt and eventually would have body hair, breasts, and then periods. He told Grandma, who we were living with, that she had to fatten me up since I did not have sufficient body fat to make those "things" happen.

When my breasts finally appeared, I was fourteen years old. I never undressed in front of Marise or anyone else. I was too ashamed to be seen naked. It was not until we moved to New York, years later, that my sisters Marise and Fifi locked the bedroom door and told me that they would not let me out until I let them take a peek at my breasts.

I looked into their eyes; they were serious. So I flashed them and ran.

My breasts were always "in the way," something that grew out of my body that I could care less about. The uncomfortable relationship with my breasts finally changed when I went to one of Dr. Christiane Northrup's lectures, during which I also met Louise Hay. Christiane mentioned in her lecture that we have to love every part of our bodies. If we do not, then something might happen to get rid of it.

When I read the book, *Heal Your Body*, which Louise gave me, the relationship with my breasts changed for the better. Now, when I look at them, I see that they are gorgeous and still hanging in there.

I see them as a part of my total self. They have been with me now for a long time, a part of my femininity, and they have brought me many sensual pleasures. When I'm naked in front of the mirror, I look at them, cup them in my hands, and tell them: "Not to worry, my friends, you are safe with me."

The first time I faced having a mammogram, I dreaded it. After the awful procedure, when a friend asked me to describe my experience, I did a show-and-tell. I took both my hands and put them on my left breast while making a squeezing motion, first up and down, then side to side. I said it was like taking two books, which have been in the freezer for a few hours, and squeezing your breasts with them. The painful procedure is something we women have to endure, if we choose to do so.

Some women, like me, resent the fact that we must deal with so much about our bodies through-out our lives.

I remind patients who voice this concern that men seem to have it easy while they are young, but soon their turn will come! They will spend their old-er years consulting with a urologist about their pros-tate and having dreaded rectal exams. Knowing this makes dealing with PMS, cramps, pelvic exams, and mammograms just a little easier!

1998 SAN DIEGO, CALIFORNIA

THE SINGING SURGEON

I was performing an abdominal hysterectomy early one morning, and we were having difficulty because the patient was bleeding profusely. The situation was so tense in that operating room that I felt I must do something, while still focusing on the patient, of course.

So, I burst into song:

"She works hard for the money ... pa dap pa dap. So hard for it honey... pa dap pa dap. She works hard for the money, so you better treat her right!"

The startled OR crew laughed, and we all took a deep breath.

I don't think they had ever experienced a surgeon break out in a song, no less a Donna Summers' disco song, while operating. (The operation was successful, by the way.)

1998: SAN DIEGO, CALIFORNIA

I FEEL YOUR PAIN!

I was at a hotel attending a seminar when I missed a step, slipped, twisted my right ankle, and fell on my right buttock. Three colleagues helped me to the lobby. One of them asked if I was trying to imitate President Clinton. Apparently, the day before, he had slipped down some stairs, torn the major tendon of his right leg, and had to undergo two hours of surgery.

By the time I reached the hotel lobby, I could not put any pressure on my right foot and just stood there watching it swell.

I was placed in a wheelchair and taken to the ER at Alvarado Hospital, where I was told that all beds were filled. One of the nurses recognized me, gave me a quick evaluation in the waiting room, and then went to see the doctor in charge. Everyone was running around like a chicken, but she was able to get the doctor's okay for me to have X-rays taken of my foot and my right buttock, which was now very painful.

I had to go to the bathroom. I summoned a young volunteer who dutifully agreed to wheel me there. By the time I got to the lady's room, my ankle was extremely swollen, and it took intense effort for me to maneuver from the wheelchair, pull down my slacks and underwear, and sit on the toilet. Being six feet tall did not help. It was painful to sit on my ass, and at the same time try not put any weight on my right foot. It was yet another ordeal to readjust my underwear and pants and get back into that wheelchair.

After finishing in the lady's room, an x-ray technician, Michael, came to wheel me to the x-ray department. I had to take all my clothes off, including my underwear, which had some metallic design on it, and my necklace, so it would not interfere with the x-rays. I had to put on two gowns, one open in the back and the other open in the front.

With Michael's help, I crawled onto the x-ray table. The table was cold, and I had to be in certain positions, which aggravated the pain. Michael then told me that usually patients came to him on a gurney because they would have already been undressed, seen by the doctor, and then sent to be x-rayed. He suggested that I at least go back to the ER on a gurney. To do so, he would have to retrieve my clothes in the bathroom. I felt so self-conscious. I had thrown my clothes and underwear on top of a basket for dirty gowns, as I had thought I would go back and get dressed on my own.

It was with embarrassment that I asked Michael to please give me my underwear so I would feel more comfortable. He put the rest of my clothes on the gurney.

When I got back to the ER, Michael had no choice but to leave me in the hallway. I spent at least an hour waiting for the doctor who was running from one bed to the next, looking at x-rays, while talking to nurses or doctors on the phone.

While I waited some of my colleagues passed by on their way to see patients. Only a couple stopped to ask what was going on. One of them, Dennis Wilcox, a surgeon, was the most compassionate. I felt so good after he spoke to me. The other doctors had been rushed, indifferent. But Dennis came close, held my hand, and stroked my forehead. I was not expecting that those small gestures would mean so much to me. For a while after he left, a calm feeling stayed with me and eased my pain.

I was finally examined by Dr. Rodriguez. My x-rays revealed that I had two avulsion fractures, one on each side of my ankle. An avulsion fracture is an injury to the bone in a location where a tendon or ligament attaches to it. As a result of physical trauma a fragment of bone tears away.

I would have to be off my feet for a while. Little did I know that it would take six months before I was completely healed.

Being less independent during that time, hobbling around, being in pain, made me think a lot about compassion. I had always been compassionate with my patients, but *being a patient* made me even more empathetic thereafter. Pain is quite an eye-opening lesson.

1998 SAN DIEGO, CALIFORNIA

A LEARNING EXPERIENCE

There was a picture in the newspaper of President Clinton standing with his crutches. After an Oval Office ceremony, he said that his torn knee tendon had been "a very humbling experience, which gave me a new respect for people with disabilities. I will never again see a person who has to deal with a disability in the same light."

I found myself learning the same lesson after breaking those two little bones in my right ankle. I had been trying to do my everyday routines with one good leg, crutches, and a walking boot.

When I was able to let go of my crutches. I was in tears. I have always been very independent, especially physically. I never had to depend on anyone for anything. I had endured cruel hours during medical school, internship, residency training, and later on during the first ten years of practice when I was busy doing both obstetrics and gynecology. I'd never felt so vulnerable in my life as when I had this ankle accident, and I had so many lessons to learn as I slowly healed.

Using a walking boot is much better than a walking cast since it can be removed to take showers and to sleep. But I always forgot to put it on when I woke up in the middle of the night to go to the bathroom! I would take a few steps and then, ouch. So I'd be in the dark, hopping on my good leg. I had no problem during the day with my boot on. But the night was another story.

So many of my patients and friends hinted or outright said that maybe the universe was trying to tell me to slow down. I was used to walking an average of six to nine miles per week for exercise, and I was also in the habit of parking as far as possible from my destination. I couldn't do that any longer. But I didn't think I led a hectic life until I tried to continue my usual routine after my injuries….

One day I just wanted to do a few simple things like go to the store and pick up computer software and a power cord, go to the bank, see a patient at the hospital, and then return home. A piece of cake, I thought, especially with the new temporary disability permit my orthopedist, Dr. Steve Orcutt, signed for me.

I'll just find myself a spot in the disabled zone close to the entrance, so I won't have to walk too far, I thought. But I didn't realize it was more complicated than that. I couldn't drive with my boot. It takes time to remove it to drive and put it on at every stop. So no hopping into the car and driving away for each errand.

When I got to the store, I found the software, but no AC power cords. A clerk suggested another store in the complex. After waiting in a short line to pay for the software, I was already tired just standing there, lopsided. When I got outside, the entrance to the other store didn't look too far away. But by the time I walked to it, found the power cord, paid for it, and returned to my car, I was exhausted and in pain.

But I didn't want to stop. I had to go to the bank and then to the hospital. I guess I could have put it off, but I felt like a sissy not being able to do these simple tasks. Fortunately, there were not too many customers at the bank. When I got to the hospital, the doctor's parking lot was a good distance from the entrance. The handicap parking by the Emergency Room was full. Finally, I parked across the street, walked through the hallways of the hospital, saw my patient, discharged her, and limped back to my car. I was a wreck.

There was a lesson for me in this experience. I have always been kind to people, especially if they are disabled. But I always walk fast, leaving people behind. I used to make a joke and say that I have long legs and if I take small steps, I'll fall!

Does my way of walking have something to do with how I see life? Am I supposed to go slower and "smell more roses"? Do you?

1998 SAN DIEGO, CALIFORNIA

YES, THEY CAN DEFLATE

Women who have breast implants are usually concerned about them rupturing during a mammogram. I have always reassured them that this is a rare occurrence, until it happened to a patient of mine named Booie. (No, not *Boobie*.)

Booie was very flat-chested before having saline implants. But she was very happy she had the procedure done. So was her husband.

Three days after she'd had one of those dreaded mammograms, she noticed her right breast getting smaller and smaller, until finally it flattened out.

She was very concerned that whatever was in the implant was being absorbed throughout her body. Her husband, trying to be a good sport, jokingly told her not to worry; she just had a flat tire and could go back to the doctor and have it pumped up again.

But Booie found out she could not just have saline re-injected into the breast. She had the choice of having the deflated implant removed and replaced with a new one OR have both implants removed and go back to being flat-chested.

I think you can guess what she chose to do.

1998 SAN DIEGO, CALIFORNIA

A SHOCKING SENILE MOMENT

Some of my patients accustomed to being in charge of their lives have come to my office complaining of forgetfulness and memory loss and I've always been sympathetic.

But I didn't realize how confusing and scary this could be until one day when I was forty-seven, a woman approached me in a store, calling me by my first name and telling me how glad she was to see me. She came over and kissed me, and said how sorry she was that I had missed her last party. I stared at her and tried in vain to remember who she was. What a weird feeling!

It took several minutes for me to remember that the woman was Marcia, a *dear friend* of mine! I was shocked that my brain had failed me in this way. It was a freaky, frightening experience. I never had trouble remembering things that happened years ago, even when I was writing one or even two books at a time. I performed major surgery and juggled many tasks with no problem for years.

But the day had now arrived where I wondered if I could totally rely on my memory for everything! I knew that loss of concentration is not from lack of estrogen alone. I used birth-control pills; I should have no lack of estrogen. The villain has got to be the aging process itself… or maybe just brain overload?

I take no chances and now use a daily planner and review it every morning. Sticky notes lie everywhere to remind me what I need to do. At my office, I leave myself reminders on the answering machine. At home, I keep a carbon-copy message book next to my answering machine, record all messages, and leave them in full view.

The shock of one memory-loss moment shook me up and changed my habits forever.

1998 SAN DIEGO, CALIFORNIA

LAUGHTER IS THE BEST MEDICINE

At my office, it was a tradition during Halloween for us to dress up. One year I turned myself into a pregnant woman. Patients, colleagues, and staff at the hospital reacted with shock: "I didn't know you were pregnant!" Then I'd show them the sign on my chest: "Seventh Fleet – One Night Stand," and we would laugh like crazy.

I "carried" my pregnancy all day. It was the first time I understood how hard it was for my pregnant patients to bend down, go to the bathroom, get in and out of a car. It was also nice to see how perfect strangers would run to assist. "Poor pregnant baby, let me help you."

The following Halloween, my assistants Pam and Krista told me I was going to be dressed as a cow, and they would be ladybugs. In the morning, I patiently sat while they painted my face black and white, and assisted me into my costume. It had an udder with four teats right over my pelvic area, and I had two horns on my head.

I practiced a little routine: when I moved my body from left to right, the udder would go the opposite way. I would then pull the teats one by one, saying, "From this one you get low-fat milk, this one whole milk, this one skim milk, and this one *chocolate* milk!" I would then shake my tail, shake the udder, and take a bow.

I would do my routine before entering each patient's examining room, and they would laugh so hard that some had tears in their eyes. So many said they needed a good laugh that day. The same thing happened when I was on my way to eat lunch across the street. As I passed by the pharmacy in my office building, I stood at the door and did my routine. "Please wait," one of the staff said as he ran to the computer and wrote on a sheet of white paper with black ink "Got Milk!" He then cut it out large enough to fit in the space below my neck and above my breasts while saying "I swear I'm not trying to be disrespectful." The whole place was in an uproar.

As I crossed the street, each person I encountered would point at me. I put on a broad smile, did my routine, and they were hysterical. I thought: There are devastating floods in Central America, the whole world is in pain, and yet with just a few seconds of my time I can bring laughter to perfect strangers. Then the idea came to me to go to the hospital, stop at the departments, and all the floors where the sick patients lay in their beds, and do my "udder routine."

"Oh my God, that's Doctor Jean-Murat, one of our doctors!" someone would say.

When I got to the x-ray department, I changed it up. I stood at the door holding my tail and said I had come for a "Moomoogram." More laughter.

When I made my grand entrance into the doctor's lounge, I received the same reaction. Each time another doctor came in someone would say, "Go Carolle, do your routine!"

On the way back to my office, I detoured across the hall to the office of Dr. Kossman, an oncologist. There were always patients receiving chemotherapy, and if anyone needed a laugh, it was them. They loved it.

Dr. Wilkinson, his partner, soon came out to see what was causing all the commotion. When he saw me, he said he wanted to take a picture of the two of us and put it on his desk so that when he referred a patient to me, they'd know that laughter would be part of their medicine!

1999 SAN DIEGO, CALIFORNIA

MIDLIFE TIME-OUT

Cynthia, a patient of mine for many years, came in for her annual exam. Just like me, she was going through what we called our "midlife crisis," and she was trying hard to cope. Suddenly, I had a brilliant idea. What about doing something spontaneous that I should have, but had never, done for myself? *What about just taking off to do nothing!*

"Are you busy tomorrow?" I asked Cynthia. When she said no she was free, I asked her to join me in a beautiful part of town called Seaport Village, *just to goof off.* She could not believe her ears.

Cynthia and I met there in the afternoon. She said she'd called all her friends to tell them she had an appointment by the ocean with her doctor to learn how to do nothing.

We headed for the outdoor Greek restaurant, and ate while giggling, like two young kids. We had two hours of free parking to kick back. We each brought a comfy blanket, so we headed to a beautiful area on the grass by the ocean and spread out, using our purses as pillows.

It was another gorgeous day in San Diego... and the only thing on our to-do list was to enjoy looking at the water, seagulls, boats and yachts, and laugh at the busy tourists.

Just what the doctor ordered.

1999 SAN DIEGO, CALIFORNIA

GOODBYE KINKY HAIR

I t can take a long time and much drama to make a change… big or small.

I was never vain but was always unhappy with my kinky black hair. I envied women with straight hair. I spent miserable hours at the hairdresser making my hair straight. But as an active woman, it wasn't easy to keep it that way.

My husband, Albert, was tired of hearing me complain that I had to cut my hair *someday*. He told me that he would love me whether it was short or long. When we would cross paths with a black woman with lovely short hair, he would make sure to remind me how I could look as beautiful as she did.

For many years I told Francoise, my hairdresser, that one day, I would find the courage to cut my hair off. "You will not find the courage to do it," she'd say. "Your hair is too beautiful. You don't have the type of face to have your hair short." Maybe the fear that I would not be attractive any longer kept me from cutting it. I came to realize a woman's hair is deeply engrained with her sexuality and how she sees herself as a woman. Her hair can ruin or save the day.

I felt beautiful with my long straight hair. I remember flying to Florida for a family reunion. They had never seen my hair looking this good, so I made sure that I had it done the day before leaving. I flew on a small plane from San Diego to Los Angeles, on my first leg to Miami. When we got to LA, I was shocked to find it was raining, and I would have to walk through it to get to the gates! I refused to get out of the plane. The poor male flight attendant finally found a large garbage bag to put over my head.

There was always an excuse not to cut my it off. "I'm doing a series of educational shows on TV and need to look the same throughout the series. I cannot have a drastic hairstyle change as I would not look like the woman on my book cover. I'll do it when I turn fifty, the time for menopause, time for change." But time went on and the right moment never came.

I made me realize how difficult it can be for people to change. Whether someone has a bad habit such as smoking, drug addiction, being in an abusive relationship, or an unfulfilling job, the fact is we stay in these situations because we are not strong enough to make changes, or we are afraid to deal with the unknown.

Jill, the editor at Hay House, called me one day to tell me that the release of my new book *Menopause Made Easy* was going to be delayed for two months. "This means you have time to cut your hair and get another professional picture for the book cover." This was also when David Christel dumped some very tough love on me. He was a friend who had worked with me on many writing projects, and had to suffer through the tantrums I had with my hairdresser. One of my projects was actually called, *"Taking Charge of Your Life."*

"Don't be a HYPOCRITE," he said. "How can you teach women to empower themselves when you can't do something as simple as cut your hair? What are you waiting for? Why not NOW?"

He was a man and a white one to boot. What did he know about a forty-eight year-old black woman struggling with kinky hair? But David's daring comments finally got through my hair to my brains. I decided it was time.

The night before I was to go to Francoise's salon, I had a horrible nightmare. I saw myself standing in front of a mirror after the haircut. I was a marine in a crew cut that was still too long. "Cut it shorter," yelled a voice. The next time I looked in the mirror, I had been beheaded. I awoke in a sweat that made me mad enough to hurry to my hairdresser.

Francoise didn't make it any easier. "I will not cut it," she told me bluntly. "Find yourself someone else." She rushed away to another customer.

How could she do this to me? A professional photographer was coming to my house that afternoon to take another picture for the book cover. I could not just go to any barber, and I also needed her to put in a relaxer, and dye the gray roots.

While I sat in the salon fuming, I realized another reason it's so difficult for people to get out of a situation they do not like: There are others around who don't want them to change, for whatever reason.

I even doubted myself. There I was, a very strong woman, born in Haiti, who overcame many obstacles to become a board-certified obstetrician and gynecologist in America, the land of opportunity, someone who had made life or death decisions. And I was agonizing over something as simple as a haircut! How could people with fewer positive experiences in their lives, with low self-esteem, or fear of financial repercussions, be able to make a painful step towards change?

As I thought about these questions, I mentally slapped my face, then grabbed Francoise and asked her to be an ally for the change I was ready for, instead of the enemy. She finally gave in. But she still held up the scissors and asked. *"Are you sure?"*

"Damn it, go ahead!" I screamed. When the scissors started to cut, it was a physical pain, like my right arm was being cut off. The first strands fell on the floor. The more she cut, the more I felt that part of me was being cut off too. It was a horrible experience.

When it was over, I was shocked to see my new look. Acceptance came slowly. From now on, this was the way I would look. No more hours waiting or fighting with Francoise. No more hair dryers.

I never let my hair grow again. I loved it short. I've even learned to cut it myself. My hair is now only a quarter-inch long. I have learned how to dye my graying roots without ruining my hair, and to put in a relaxer to soften my hair when I want to.

Free at last!

1999: JACMEL, HAITI

BACK TO MY HOMELAND

On June 30, 1999, I performed my last surgery at Grossmont Hospital because I could no longer afford my overhead with ever-increasing malpractice insurance premiums.

I decided to join Dr. Charles René, a fellow obstetrician and gynecologist from Haiti who resided in New Orleans. Dr. René had been going back to Haiti three times a year for over fourteen years to provide outpatient care and minor surgeries to the poor. His dedicated team helps hundreds of patients a day, working twelve or more hours.

I decided to join his team. It was time to go home!

To get to La Vallée de Jacmel in the Southeastern region of Haiti, we flew into Port-au-Prince and took the two-lane paved road going south. At a steep point, when looking back we could see the Atlantic Ocean, and looking forward, the Caribbean Sea. If we continued straight towards the ocean, we would end up in Jacmel, a popular destination because of its beauty and distance from the political turmoil that plagued Port-au-Prince.

A mile before we got to Jacmel, we started another arduous climb on another unpaved bumpy road. But these rough roads were dear to me. I could not stop crying when it really hit me that I was *home*. And returning, as I dreamed so long ago, capable of making a difference in the lives of my people.

A short history lesson about my homeland:

Haiti and Jacmel have a prominent place in the history of the world. The Haitian national anthem La Dessalinienne was named after one of the leaders of the Haitians' independence from France, Jean-Jacques Dessalines. He was a freed slave, served as an officer in the French army when the colony was trying to withstand Spanish and British incursions, but later became a commander in the revolt against France.

Toussaint L'Ouverture, the leader of the Haitian revolution, an astute former slave renowned for his military genius and political acumen, laid the groundwork that prepared Haiti to become the second independent republic in the Americas. Before he died in a French prison, Toussaint Louverture wrote: "By overthrowing me, you have killed only the trunk of the tree of liberty of the black people; but it will grow back by the roots, for they are deep and numerous."

Toussaint was replaced by Dessalines, who led the first successful attempt by a slave population in the Americas and the world to win independence from European colonialism. Dessalines was the leader of the last assault in the Battle of Vertières in 1803, defeating French troops sent by Napoleon, declaring Haiti an independent nation in 1804. He was chosen by a council of generals made up of blacks and mulattos to assume the office of Governor-General. In September 1804, he proclaimed himself Emperor and ruled in that capacity until being assassinated in 1806.

General Francisco de Miranda, born in Venezuela in 1750, played an important role during the Spanish American wars of independence, successfully liberating a vast portion of South America. General Magloire Ambroise, born in Jacmel in 1774, fought with Dessalines for the independence of Haiti and was one of the generals who signed the Independence Act in 1806. At the orders of Dessalines, he was the one who Francisco de Miranda contacted when he went to Haiti looking for help. He gave Miranda munitions and men to fight the Spaniards. Miranda designed the first Venezuelan flag near Jacmel and first raised it on March 12, 1806. This day is still celebrated as Venezuelan Flag Day.

Later on, Simón Bolívar, also born in Venezuela in 1783, was a military and political leader who played a pivotal role in Hispanic America's successful struggle for independence from the Spanish Empire. In 1815, after an attempt was made on his life, wounded, he fled to Haiti, where he was granted sanctuary and protection. In 1817, on the condition that he would abolish slavery, with Haitian soldiers and vital material support, Bolívar returned to Venezuela.

While treating the patients in La Vallée, I had to learn how to take cold showers again, quickly cleaning only places where you sweat. First you soap, then you scream, as you quickly rinse that area with cold water!

Remembering the long difficult history of Haiti, and my long difficult journey to become a surgeon, I screamed… *"For the love of my country…for the love of my country…for the love of my country!!"*

1999 SAN DIEGO, CALIFORNIA

SEX AND THE MATURE WOMAN

Mother told me, "What I liked the most about menopause was that you did not have any more periods, there was no more fear of pregnancy, and the sex was better!" This has been confirmed by all the post-menopausal Haitian women I have interviewed.

One of my Haitian friends, who is over eighty years old and wishes to remain anonymous, told me that up until the week before her husband's death from a long illness, she made sure that her sex life was satisfactory. After he died, she made soup with okra, hoping that it would cool off her fiery desire.

But it didn't work! A friend suggested some tea made with aloe, which worked somewhat. Her only recourse was frequent showers. Her children and grandchildren could not understand why she was taking so many showers!

Carol, an eighty-year-old new patient, presented the same problem to me during a consultation. She explained that she needed help with something entirely private; she even got up and made sure that no one was in the hallway and that the door of my office was closed tight. In a whisper, she confided that she wanted to have sex all the time, which must mean that something was wrong with her! Carol had been married to the same man for sixty years but was now a widow. During the ten years before his death, her husband had been impotent.

Carol recently had a wild fling with a forty-year-old virile man. They broke off shortly afterward, leaving Carol in a predicament. All her male friends were old and married. The few young men she knew were not attracted to her. She felt lost. Carol also explained that her Catholic upbringing, her pride, and the fear of catching a sexually transmitted disease would not allow her to participate in a sexual encounter with a male prostitute. What was she to do?

Carol was hoping that I could give her a pill to diminish her desire. I told her that there was no such pill!

Instead, I had a very open discussion with her about masturbation, vibrators, and sex toys. I explained there were stores that carried many such items.

As Carol was leaving my office, she asked if she could give me a hug, during which she whispered in my ear: "I'm on my way to get a wig and dark glasses, and then find one of those stores!"

1999 SAN DIEGO, CALIFORNIA

SEX PRESCRIPTIONS

One month following a vaginal hysterectomy, my patient, Judy, left a message to have me call her right away. She had followed my advice not to have intercourse for four weeks post-surgery, but her husband had been complaining almost daily about their lack of intimacy. Judy couldn't understand this. Her husband was in his fifties, and she thought he would have cooled off by now.

They had been at a restaurant when he realized that the four-week moratorium was over. He said to a startled Judy, "Finish up, we have to hurry home!" Judy's husband was usually a very careful driver, but that night he drove like he was in the Indianapolis 500.

After they got cozy and romantic in their bedroom, he looked disappointed. "I felt like I was hitting a rock in there," he complained.

As Judy explained his reaction to me on the phone, I wondered if one of her sutures might have hardened, so I asked her to come in for a look.

When I examined the vaginal vault with the help of a speculum, I saw that it was healing very well. There was only a small remnant of a suture, which was very soft.

I told Judy that her husband's experience could be due to the continuing scarring and healing process. Then I pulled out my pad and wrote a prescription *for him.*

Her husband's prescription read: "PLEASE BE PATIENT."

Eventually, I heard from Judy that the "hard as a rock" sensation went away with time, and that she and her husband were *both* enjoying a great sex life.

2000 SAN DIEGO, CALIFORNIA

EMBRACING MENOPAUSE

I would be turning fifty this year. Since my mother went through menopause at that age, I assumed my turn would be soon. I looked forward to menopause! This longing started after my first menstrual cramp, and continued when friends, patients, and I myself, got very tired of PMS symptoms. I couldn't wait till the day those "periods" stopped!

When I asked my mother about menopause, she had told me that what she liked best was that there were no more periods, no more fear of pregnancy and that sex was better. What a deal!

However, when I asked my white, middle-class, pre-menopausal patients what they thought about menopause, a good majority said they expected a time of hardship, which should be controlled with medical and other intervention.

In my Haitian culture, aging is associated with knowledge and wisdom. I grew up looking forward to growing older and being like my Grandma – beautiful, wise, loved, and respected. The opposite is true in the American culture, where aging is associated with "deteriorating" both mentally and physically. Many of my patients dread the idea of growing old. No one believes me when I tell them that I look forward to going through menopause, and being a wise older woman!

In Haitian culture, youngsters have no voice until they grow up. It did not matter that I was a board-certified obstetrician and gynecologist in my thirties. Mother and Grandma told me that my obstetrical opinion did not count, even though I had all the diplomas.

However, as I racked up more birthdays and living experience, I was more respected and accepted. And so, I was never afraid of getting older, menopause, or its symptoms.

More than seventy-five percent of women experience hot flashes during the first few months of menopause, and almost half still have them after five years. Some in their sixties still experience them to some degree. Other women have no symptoms at all, or the symptoms are so mild that the women don't realize they're entering menopause until their periods cease.

An unfortunate forty percent of menopausal women suffer from debilitating hot flashes and seek medical treatment like hormone replacement.

"The only way I feel better when I have hot flashes is to stick my head into the refrigerator," says Rosemary, a colleague, who remembered her first hot flash. It happened when she was at a function, sipping some red wine, and began to turn as red as the wine.

Menopause means the end of a woman's menstrual cycle. Even if there are some temporary hot flashes, or other symptoms that might need therapy, it's still just an inevitable stage in our lives through which we all pass on the road to becoming more respected "wise women."

It helps to have a sense of humor about it…A friend of mine just entering the menopausal stages, hated to move from CA to Alaska when her husband got transferred. Months later, I received a call from her. She missed San Diego but explained that her being in Alaska during menopause had a definite upside: "When I get hot flashes, I'm quite comfortable in the cold Alaskan weather."

2001 SAN DIEGO, CALIFORNIA

WHENEVER I TAKE A LEAK, I THINK OF YOU

I had heard that Dr. Richard Philpot, a fifty-year-old colleague, was going to have his second bypass surgery and there was concern he might not make it. I was in the doctor's lounge at Alvarado Hospital when the severity of his illness was confirmed by Dr. Elia, his cardiologist.

Dr. Philpott was a kind man, and wonderful surgeon, who always teased me after I joined the staff as the first woman. He called me "The Voodoo Doctor," followed by his humming the *Twilight Zone* theme. I laughed but would remind him over and over that Voodoo, contrary to what Hollywood portrayed, is an indigenous healing religion like many others, and that my grandfather, a respected Voodoo priest, was one of the most effective healers I had ever known.

I was very grateful to Dr. Philpott, who was one of the few doctors to genuinely welcome me to the staff, and occasionally would help me with difficult deliveries if I asked. He'd say, "Of course my Voodoo Doctor, anything to make you happy."

Now I wanted to help *him*, so I told Dr. Elia I wanted to do some healing techniques for Dr. Philpott. I could see the skepticism in his eyes, but he agreed our colleague needed all the help he could get. "Could I charge for the visit?" I asked jokingly. "I don't think they'd reimburse you for it," he answered with a laugh.

When I got to Dr. Philpott's room, his wife and a friend were visiting, so I asked if they would leave me alone with him. He was lying in bed, obviously in pain, his skin a grayish color. "This is your Voodoo Doctor coming to do her healing ritual," I said, pulling up a chair to sit on his left side.

I asked him to close his eyes as I massaged his hand. I told him to visualize his heart as a reservoir, and the damaged blood vessels that were clogged as the pipes that brought water into his sink. The diseased "pipes" were going to be replaced with others from his leg. From then on, he should visualize them as open, open, open, bringing perfect blood flow to his heart.

I also showed him how to breathe to help his pain. All this time I was holding his left hand. "Throughout your surgery I'll be there with you in spirit, from the time they take you to the holding area you will feel my presence and a slight pressure on your hand, just like now."

As I was talking and massaging his hand, Dr. Philpott listened and went along with me, breathing as I suggested. Soon, I could see his pain was eased and that the grayish look was getting a little pinker.

Two weeks later, I was shocked to see him walking in the parking lot!

When he saw me, he laughed hysterically.

"You wouldn't believe what happened, Carolle. The surgery went well, even though they had difficulty getting my heart working again. Then, after they removed the Foley catheter, I wasn't able to pee. The nurse suggested I go into the shower and let the water run. I was feeling very uncomfortable and hated the idea of having to put the catheter back in. That was when I thought of you Carolle, my Voodoo Doctor."

I hugged him as he continued. "I remembered you taught me to keep the blood vessels in my heart working by saying "open… open." So, as the water was running in the bathroom, I concentrated on my bladder sphincter and said open, open, open… and all of a sudden, I was peeing. So, my dear Carolle, whenever I take a leak, I think of you!"

2006 HEIDELBERG, GERMANY

PLAYING NANNY

My little brother Jacky joined the Air Force and was the only sibling of mine who did not choose a healthcare career. We told him he was going to be a bachelor until he died, until one day he met Marayda, a beautiful, sweet young lady whose parents were from Puerto Rico. It was love at first sight for all of us.

They married, got stationed in Germany, and Marayda was getting ready to give birth to their first child. My sisters Massou, Marise, and Fifi, my brother Lesly and his wife Louana, and I had a teleconference call to decide who would go to Germany to help out. Mother had established a cherished family custom of being present when one of her grandchildren was born, wherever that was in the world, and then spend the first few weeks cooking, cleaning, and babysitting so that the mother could just breastfeed and rest.

It didn't take long to figure out that I was the new designated "Grandma." Even though I'd never had children of my own, I'd delivered hundreds, had a more flexible schedule and was now the matriarch of the family.

"Now Carolle, don't run away when it's time to change diapers," I was told.

We all laughed, remembering how, during family reunions, they would all point to me when one of the babies needed a diaper change. I had no choice but to promise my family that, yes, I would go, and yes, I would change diapers and have pictures taken for proof!

The part I didn't like was going to a country for the first time in the middle of winter, where people smoked everywhere, and where I didn't speak the language. Well, I could always use sign language and let my fingers do the walking/talking, remembering a hospital patient I helped who needed instructions, but spoke only Russian.

When I flew to Frankfurt, my brother's beautiful daughter Zoe was only a few days old, and it was a great feeling to hold her in my arms. I did not realize that newborns take so much energy out of their mothers, especially if they are breastfeeding. As promised, I changed diapers, held Zoe to rock her to sleep, and cooked their favorite foods with extra portions that I put in Ziploc bags and plastic containers to store in the freezer. I did my best to be the perfect "Grandma."

We were staying not too far from Heidelberg, one of the warmest regions of Germany. Even during the winter, it was still beautiful. Nanny Carolle had a chance to do some sightseeing, visit a castle, and eat gelato at the only smoke-free café along the Rhine River.

It was interesting that wherever we went, I saw placards and signs of different sizes with the word *Ausfahrt* and an arrow pointing away from it. "It seems every road here leads to *Ausfahrt*," I commented to my brother, who nodded and smiled.

When it was time for me to finally leave Germany, he presented me with a souvenir T-shirt that read, *Where the Hell is Ausfahrt?*

Laughing, he said, "Carolle, the word *Ausfahrt* means EXIT."

2008 DELRAY BEACH, FLORIDA

IT'S GOOD FOR YOU!

After a phone consultation, I befriended Jill Ann Schneider, a beautiful Jewish woman slightly older than me, who was diagnosed with cervical cancer in her twenties, but had refused to have surgery.

Instead, she changed her lifestyle drastically and pursued an intensive study of alternative healing practices. She also took off for four months to hike in the Andes Mountains of Peru, instead of following the medical protocols. When she returned from her "healing vacation," the cancer was gone, and two years later, she birthed her only child, Aaron.

Jill went on to develop a holistic coaching and detoxification program, customized for each person, which includes juice fasting, eating living and raw foods, integrative massage, shiatsu and deep tissue bodywork, and restorative yoga.

Jill Ann Schneider became my holistic life coach, and each year, around the holidays, I would do a one-on-one retreat week with her in Delray Beach, Florida. What I especially appreciated was her caring manner, lovely smile, and ability to lay me down on a mat and walk on my aching back.

Part of my regimen was to take a lukewarm coffee enema lying on the bathroom floor on my left side, and holding it in until I felt I was going to explode. "It's good for you! It's good for you …you need to get rid of all the toxins you've been accumulating in your body," she would say.

As I lay on her floor panting, I remembered the days when Grandma, before the school year started in Haiti, would give my sister and me a purgative made of crushed leaves mixed with a homemade castor oil, and then an enema the next day. What came out while squatting on the latrine, could be felt – slimy little worms that made you cringe, while you screamed your head off.

Grandma would say it was *good for us*: "You have to get rid of these little creatures so they will not eat up your brains and keep you from learning at school!"

2009 STILLWATER, MINNESOTA

FIT FOR A QUEEN

A few months before my sixtieth birthday I went to New York. On my return to San Diego, the plane stopped in Minneapolis and a gentleman sat down next to me. With a nice smile he looked at me and said, "When I awoke this morning I felt I was going to meet someone special; I think it's you."

We chatted and I found out Gary Dalek lived in Somerset, Wisconsin, about thirteen miles from Stillwater, Minnesota. He had been working in the healing arts for twenty-eight years as a respiratory therapist, emergency medical technician, clinical hypnotherapist, and Thought Field Therapist. We both agreed our meeting was a "divine appointment," and we exchanged business cards.

Within a few weeks I received a message from Gary saying, "There's going to be a two-day expo at the Hyatt Regency Minneapolis. I have arranged for us to be featured speakers for two workshops called: *Is It My Hormones or Something Else – True Healing for a Lifetime.* This is a good way to promote yourself and your center, Carolle. We can combine your expertise in identifying the root causes of symptoms to facilitate healing with Thought Field Therapies, to alleviate negative emotions by tapping the energy points of the body. I'll arrange for your reservations."

On Friday, November 13th, I arrived in Minneapolis and was met by Gary and his assistant. We checked into the Hyatt where the Expo would take place. Gary and I worked seamlessly setting up the booth and hanging our banner. What was truly amazing was that we created the seminars and presented two successful workshops without a rehearsal. The response from the participants was very positive.

After the seminar, Gary looked at me with a mischievous smile; "I have made arrangements for you to stay in the quaint little town of Stillwater at the Water Street Inn. I'm taking you there because you have to wake up on your birthday in a place fit for a queen. In the morning go to your balcony and watch the sunrise. Then I will pick you up at 9 AM to go meet Pamela at the Stillwater Healing Center. Something tells me you two should meet."

My special abode for the night in the city of Stillwater was built in 1890 as a lumber exchange, and was preserved to keep its historical character. It opened as an Inn in 1995, nestled into the bluffs of the St. Croix River, one of America's protected Wild and Scenic Waterways.

When I awoke in the morning, I looked around my suite, which was indeed fit for a queen. From my balcony I had the most breathtaking view. Across the street I saw a pretty park next to the St. Croix River. Across the river was a mountain shaped like a cup upside down on a saucer, located in the state of Wisconsin. To the right was the Stillwater Bridge, bathed in the morning mist with cars slowly heading west to Minnesota with their headlights on. As time went by, the sun that had been hiding behind the mountain slowly came up to brighten the sky. I understood now why they called it Stillwater. As I gazed on its smooth surface, only the sparkle of sunlight reflecting off the water gave a hint of its movement as it gently flowed south. I was so thankful for the gifts of life on this very special birthday, I could not hold back my tears of joy.

Gary arrived to take me up the street to meet Pamela at the Stillwater Healing Center. She was a beautiful lady with short red hair, in her forties, who worked as a family therapist and offered Reiki Psychotherapy. Gary left us and we sat in her comfortable office.

"Gary feels we should talk. What should we talk about?" I asked her.

"I'm not sure," she replied. I reached out and grabbed her hands, looked into her eyes and said, "I'm an intuitive reader, would you like me to tell you what I see?"

"Yes," she said. I could feel we were connecting spiritually. Looking into Pamela's eyes was like taking a trip to her beautiful inner soul, with her permission. She asked a few questions about her health, family, career, and her next trip out of the country. While she talked, it was like traveling at her side; going everywhere she went. As she continued to ask questions, I answered them until there were no more. Our spiritual trip was over, but we both smiled brightly at the wonderful connection we'd made, and how much we'd covered in only *ten minutes*.

Gary wanted to show me around. As we crossed the Stillwater Bridge into Wisconsin, I asked him to please stop so I could set foot again in the state of Wisconsin. I thought back to the years I had lived there, a flood of warm memories filling my mind; memories of working to complete my post-graduate training, and the gift of the many challenges that helped shape my future. I remembered the winter when I was freezing and asking myself what a warm-blooded Haitian bush woman was doing here.

I came back into the moment. Nature's beauty filled my senses with joy. We continued on our journey, arriving at Gary's country home overlooking a lake, on forty rolling acres of land. We spent a magical day walking the land, visiting the chickens living in a 1907 hand-hewn barn, meditating in a garden with thousands of perennial flowers filling the landscape. This was indeed a celebration of life on my birthday.

As Gary was treating me to lunch before driving me to the airport, I thanked him for my wonderful visit and our collaboration at the Expo. Surprising us both, I suddenly blurted, "Do you realize how much money I would have made if I had offered intuitive readings, lasting ten minutes like Pamela's, at the Expo!"

2015 SAN DIEGO, CALIFORNIA

IMAGINE A LITTLE BLACK GIRL

On a warm summer day, I received an e-mail from a friend telling me how lucky I was to have a pool to jump into in my backyard. I burst out laughing, then sent her the following response:

> My dear friend,
> Yes, I'm lucky, but here are a few things you don't know about me...

> Imagine a little black girl raised on a humid island, who has very kinky hair that can only

be managed by pressing it with a hot comb, especially if it has gotten wet. So, swimming in any water or singing in the rain is a no-no.

When she was eight, she went to the beach for the first time and stepped on a type of fish in the water with spikes that stuck in her feet for a month, making her walk with an embarrassing limp.

She grew up secretly dreaming of *becoming a man* only so she could just go to a barber because she hated messing with her hair that grew like a weed.

She also wondered about turning into a white woman, able to take a shower, wash her hair, let it hang and dry by itself and ZAP; she's ready. But this, too, was impossible. Also, she learned that white women some-times have bad hair days.

Eventually she found some solace in real-izing that her kinky hair came packaged with beautiful, forever-young skin as she grows old, while white friends her age would look like prunes – unless they kept up on their facelifts and Botox injections.

Then came messing with Jerry Curl, and hair relaxers. But the adult with the little bush girl inside still looked at the ocean or pool as nature's gift to see and enjoy, *not something to jump into.*

Years later, she bought a house with a pool. What was she thinking? She liked the house because of the way it wrapped around the pool that she could LOOK AT from every room.

The only time she got in the pool was when someone threw her in during a wild party, ruining her hair, while everyone laughed hysterically!!!

Her favorite quote is: *"How can I take charge of my life if I can't manage my hair!"*

After plowing through every hardship and years of training to become a doctor and a surgeon, she still agonized about her hair for YEARS and couldn't make the decision to cut it.

At age forty-eight she finally bit the bullet and had it all cut off, REALLY short, for good.

Did she then jump in the ocean or into her own pool? NOPE, the water is too cold! Nice warm showers are preferred.

So, let me know when you'd like to swim in my pool to cool off, and I'll be very happy to watch from the patio.

Love, Carolle

ABOUT THE AUTHOR

Dr. Carolle Jean-Murat, MD, is a board-certified obstetrician and gynecologist, primary care specialist,
intuitive and spiritual healer, motivational speaker,
and writer. She was born into a family of shamans,
herbalists, healers, and midwives in Haiti and was
formally educated at renowned universities in Haiti,
Jamaica, Mexico, and the United States. This broad
base of knowledge enriched her practice and led her
to focus on her patients' overall well-being.

Dr. Carolle ran a successful private practice in
San Diego for over twenty years. She then opened
the Dr. Carolle Wellness & Retreat Center of San
Diego and a nonprofit charity, the Health through
Communications Foundation. Throughout her career, she has focused on serving the underprivileged,
including wounded warriors in the United States

and the people of Haiti. She strives to empower her patients and guide them to become their best selves.

For more information, visit Dr. Carolle's website at www.DrCarolle.com.

OTHER BOOKS BY DR. CAROLLE

Forgiving Yourself & Others: How to Unleash Your Future by Freeing Yourself from Past Traumas
Unresolved childhood issues are one of the major causes of unhappiness and dis-ease. Learn how healing unloving or hurtful relationships with others and with ourselves is the most crucial step we can take in our lives. http://www.drcarolle.com/store/

Heal Your Life: 25 Ways to Unleash Your Innate Healing Powers by Finding Your Purpose and Connecting with a Higher Power
We are all on a spiritual journey, and the strength of our faith and our belief in a higher power has a direct impact on our physical and mental well-being. I take you through 25 steps to strengthen your relationship with your higher power, take better care

of yourself, create healthy boundaries in all areas of life, practice forgiveness, give from the heart, and have a connection with nature to lighten stress, sorrows, and your heart. http://geni.us/healyourlife

A Day in the Life of a Healer – Short Story Series Book 2 of 4*: Daily Miracles*

Throughout her life and work as a healer around the world Dr. Carolle has been blessed with many miracles. This book shares some of the most amazing stories, proving that miracles large and small indeed do happen... and that they can happen for you.

A Day in the Life of a Healer – Short Story Series Book 3 of 4: *Just One Day*

Dr. Carolle started her journal when she was fifteen years old, writing about precious moments and important milestones when living in Haiti, Mexico, Jamaica, and the US. These stories will inspire you to dream big, and will empower you to overcome the many obstacles on your journey, so that you too can attain and enjoy your fullest life potential.

A Day in the Life of a Healer – Short Story Series Book 4 of 4: *Angels Along the Way*

Dr. Carolle's big dreams of a useful happy life began in a humble background in Haiti, one of the world's poorest countries. Overcoming enormous obstacles, she achieved the successes she hoped for as a little girl, with determination and hard work, and something more – 'earth angels', as she calls them, who encouraged her to keep going. From them she learned patience, perseverance, gratefulness, and much more. It is her hope that reading this book will inspire you to find your own encouraging, loving, life-altering 'earth angels'

www.ingramcontent.com/pod-product-compliance
Lightning Source LLC
LaVergne TN
LVHW011230080426
835509LV00005B/415